Exploring Azeroth
Islands & Isles

Thaedris,

I hope you have used the short time since you joined my household to familiarize yourself with the many duties of a steward, for I am about to set you the most difficult of all possible tasks. It has been long—far too long—since my wedding to Lor'themar, and we've yet to have a honeymoon. Two years may seem like little to those such as us, but I think of all my staff, you most understand how absence warps days to eons.

Thus, in this time of peace, I will take my chance to be absent from my duties—and from the Broken Isles—so that I can enjoy some uninterrupted time with my husband. (If I must drag him from his city of Silvermoon by one ear, so be it!) It will be your task to see that I am not bothered with anything short of a world-shattering emergency. Though you are the newest of my stewards, I trust your wisdom when it comes to judging what constitutes a truly urgent matter.

Your service is greatly appreciated.

Thalyssra

My beloved:

The city air, betimes so flush with secrets, with blood
With betrayal waiting breathless to be loosed
Hangs now silent, host only to that thud
Of a longing heart and restless thoughts.
The wind calls, the waves call, whispering sweetly
Of a bright star dancing radiant in the western sky
Waiting patiently for the clouds to pass completely
So her light might guide the long-strayed home.
Joy is birthed in the end of long separation
The passing storm brings peace and renewal
A ship pushed ever westward in its last afflations
Soon to rest in that bright horizon—soon.

Lor'themar

World of Warcraft

Exploring Azeroth
Islands & Isles

ALEX ACKS

TITAN BOOKS

My love,

I can think of no better nor more welcome surprise to know that you are on your way to the Broken Isles—and to have it delivered in your well-crafted verse is a balm for a heart that's been aching.

I know your lines well enough to see between them, and I must disagree with one strut in your poem's framework. I've lived in Suramar my entire life, and almost solely in the city that I now run for the last ten thousand years. I say this with all the love in my heart, but I am not honeymooning with you where every messenger and petty politician will have no qualm interrupting moments even more intimate than an exchange of poetry.

I shall await you eagerly in Astravar Harbor, where after a suitable embrace, we will get right back on the ship that bore you to me and find somewhere else to go where we can enjoy each other's company—and hopefully glimpse these lands healed in part by our efforts.

Your Thalyssra

My bright star,

I'll admit, I'm a little surprised you were so vehement about wanting to leave Suramar. Love has a way of making old things new, does it not? I thought to come to you mostly as a surprise, and out of a selfish desire to not be on tenterhooks while I waited for you to make your way to Silvermoon. It seems to me that the where is unimportant when all that matters is the who. When we are together, everything we could possibly need is already present.

Let us speak on it more when I arrive—once there's breath for speaking! You can tell me then where you wish to go instead.

With all my love,
Lor'themar

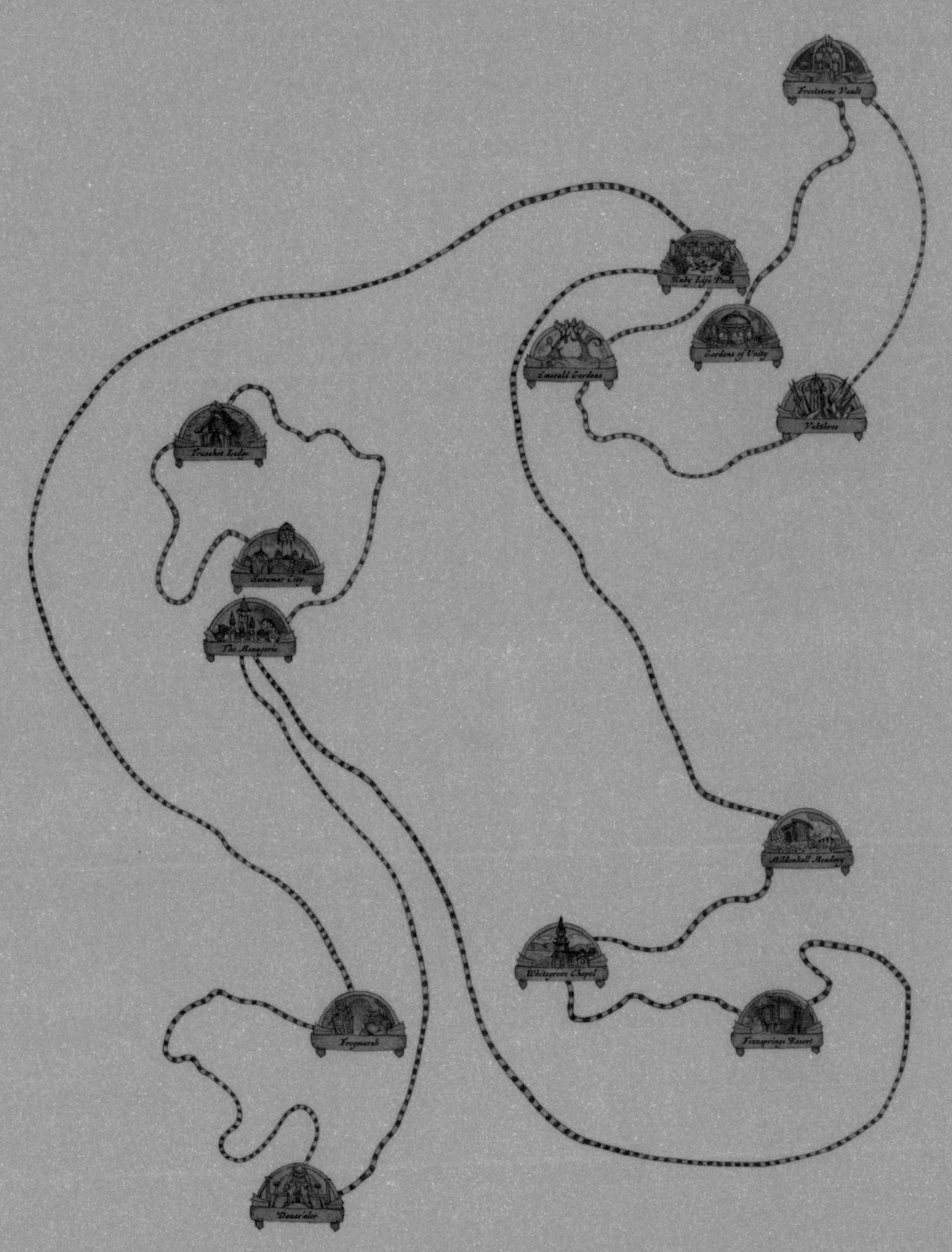

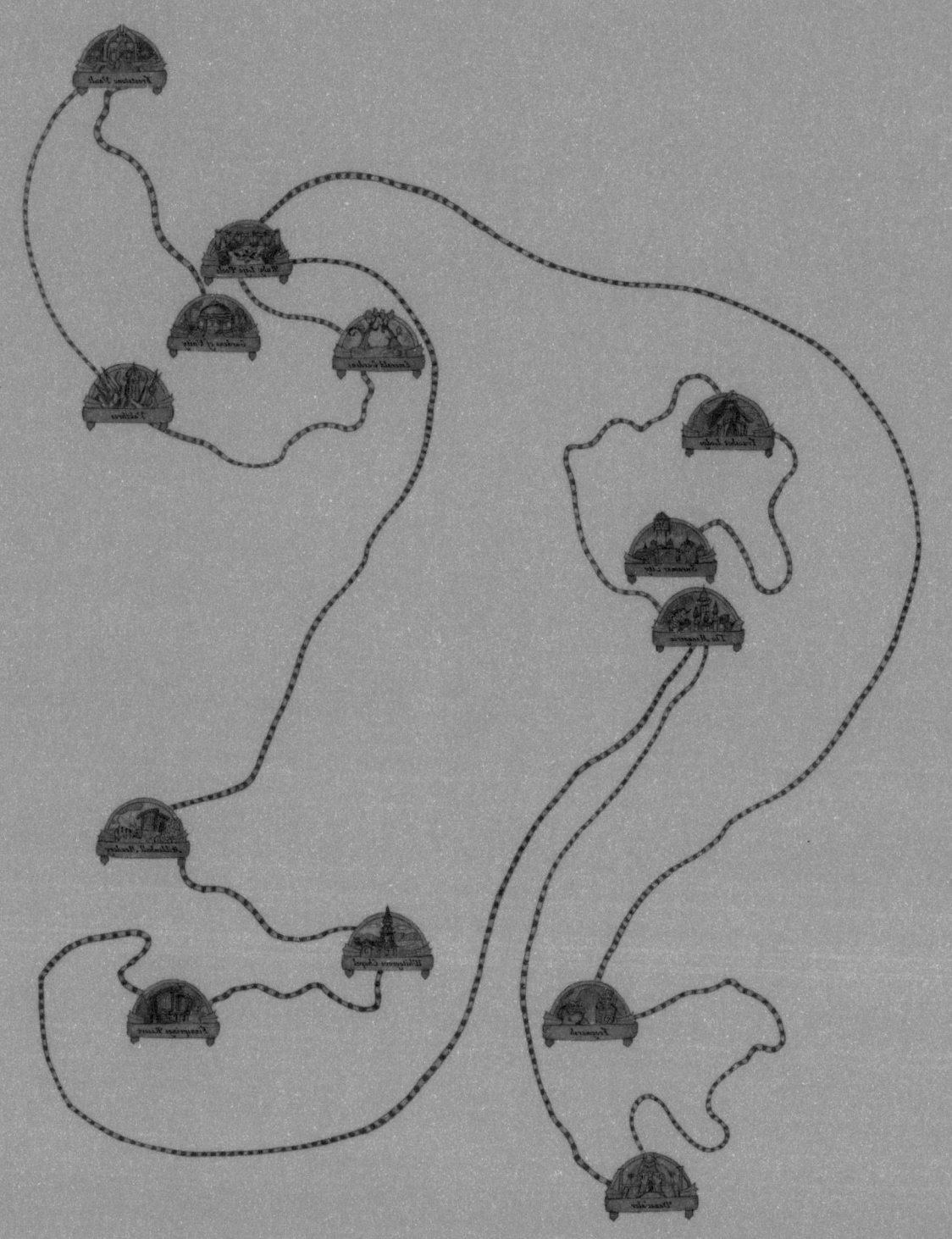

⇾ BROKEN ISLES ⇽

–I–
SURAMAR
12

AZSUNA
18

THE BROKEN SHORE
23

–II–
VAL'SHARAH
26

HIGHMOUNTAIN
36

–III–
STORMHEIM
42

DALARAN
49

⇾ ZANDALAR ⇽

–IV–
ZULDAZAR
56

VOL'DUN
71

–V–
NAZMIR
80

↣ KUL TIRAS ↢

-VI-
TIRAGARDE SOUND
92

-VII-
DRUSTVAR
106

-VIII-
STORMSONG VALLEY
116

MECHAGON
127

↣ DRAGON ISLES ↢

-IX-
THE WAKING SHORES
134

-X-
OHN'AHRAN PLAINS
142

-XI-
THE AZURE SPAN
152

-XII-
THE FORBIDDEN REACH
160

ZARALEK CAVERN
167

-XIII-
THALDRASZUS
172

⤚ BROKEN ISLES ⤙

The Broken Isles have been my home since before they were islands at all. Even torn by the destruction of the Great Sundering, the land holds much of the variety and beauty that marked it before it was broken. Deep forests, the steep and jagged peaks of mountains, wave-beaten shores . . . all of it stark and wild, overtaking the ruins of where my people once lived before retreating to Suramar City.

I know every inch of it, though if I am honest on this page, not as well as I once did. I might wish to see what is new and different, but perhaps it has been long enough—and I've been the leader of the nightborne long enough—that what is old will become new when I look at it with fresh eyes.

I suppose it will give me something to do while I wait for Lor'themar's ship to arrive. Preserving my observations here will give me something to share with my love amid our voyage to follow.

–I–
SURAMAR

As a honeymoon destination goes, one could do far worse than Suramar. My home was once the jewel of the night elven empire, but the Legion's first invasion led us to languish ten millennia beneath a magical barrier. With the Legion now thrice expelled from Azeroth, the sun shines on Suramar anew: My people bask in its gaze, dance beneath the moons. Even now, some years on, I still see them stop to marvel over gentle rainfall or a sudden storm. I'll not claim that this alone has restored our city—wounds left by civil war are not so easily healed—but the sun, the stars, the *weather* are no small sign that Suramar has entered a new era. Some reminder that we are not alone, but part of the wide world again.

Thankfully, justice has long since been brought to those who sided with former Grand Magistrix Elisande, and every nightborne has had a chance to taste the fruit of the arcan'dor. It has taken much work, relentless diplomacy, and a few well-placed threats, but no one starves for arcane magic in the streets.

The Lunastre Estate always leaves me a bit wistful, remembering the day of our wedding, and I smile like a fool about it. But isn't the point of a honeymoon to hide away from a ceremony for privacy? There's precious little of that for me in this city. And ... though I'm not one to dwell on the pains of the past, it is still too fresh to come upon the Waning Crescent and think of the people Elisande slaughtered. While I'll feel nothing but joy welcoming Lor'themar at the harbor, it's where many more of my people were sent to be turned into fuel for the Legion's soul engines ...

No, I cannot relax here, not truly. Lor'themar could write me a verse or two about time mending the pain of darker days, but that isn't the point. In Suramar if I poke a toe out of my door, I am First Arcanist Thalyssra, from whom certain duties, behaviors, attentions are expected. I want new memories that are wholly mine and Lor'themar's, **not** old ones with a Lor'themar-shaped footnote appended.

THE MENAGERIE

With so much time before Lor'themar arrives, I decided to venture afield rather than stewing in discontent and longing. I've never been one to remain still, anyway—I always studied best walking with a book. (I ought to admit that to Lor'themar one of these days. He will find it amusing.)

Before leaving, however, I stopped at my favorite place in the city. The animals in the Menagerie were once tamed with magic but are now allowed to live in a more natural state at the request of the druid Nighteyes. I stopped last at Su'esh's enclosure. I have had a fondness for the devilsaur since I heard of her running amok through Suramar during the civil war, crushing demons underfoot and shattering windows with her roar. Lor'themar liked the great beast before he'd even heard that story—he said we shared a likeness. I am still not certain how to take that.

Charming, my love. The word you want is "charming."

But leaning against the fence of her enclosure, I couldn't help but notice how small she looked at a distance, how safe to gaze upon when she wasn't roaring down the avenues with blood staining her chin. While I have no desire to literally feast upon my enemies, I feel . . . a kinship with Su'esh now. *First Arcanist*, *leader*, these are honors, but they are also their own sorts of enclosures.

I wonder where Su'esh would wish to go if I freed her.

ARMOR ASIDE: LEGACY OF AZJ'AQIR

My feelings toward warlocks are complex. I cannot deny my strong disdain for those who employ fel magic—in fact, we severed all ties from their kind after discovering their use of demons to achieve their own ends. Seeing them command fel creatures so like the ones used to hunt and punish my people isn't a sight I find at all comforting. And this set of gear of theirs, named after Azj'Aqir, the aqir empire that once sought to wipe out all life unlike itself . . . I wonder why such a name was chosen. A reminder? A cautionary tale? I hope so.

SHAL'ARAN

Ranging beyond the well-tended gardens of the Grand Promenade and out into the wilds came as something of a relief. I still recall when Suramar extended far beyond her current borders, before the barrier was erected and everything outside was left to ruin. Free of our self-imposed cage, the nightborne have begun to sprawl back out again. There are travelers on the roads, people gathering herbs and mushrooms in the forests—I even saw a youth sitting on a ruined wall and sketching the remains of one of Suramar's buildings, a picnic lunch waiting at their feet (along with a short sword). The spread of the city is slow, since there are still withered hiding in the thickets who need either help at recovery or a gentle easing from that horrifying half life.

It was natural enough for my feet to take me to Shal'Aran, my second home. I chose to walk there to breathe the free air and enjoy the journey without the hunger for the Nightwell gnawing me to pieces. The crevice that leads into Shal'Aran is a bit cleaner than it once was, but no wider—a tunnel between unlife and life, with the arcan'dor waiting at one end, its boughs heavy with fruit to free yet more nightborne from hunger.

Farodin was there when I arrived, watching over the arcan'dor like an anxious hen with her chick. Shal'Aran itself was not as quiet as I had expected it to be. Lothrius was riding herd on a small group of younger nightborne and a few night elf druids—and happier than I've seen him in some time. The first batch of new recruits, he told me, for the rebuilt Moon Guard. Shal'Aran makes an excellent new stronghold for their ranks, I feel. Best to have more than Farodin standing watch over the arcan'dor.

An image that deserves its own poem—such sentiment does it carry. I look forward to reading it one day.

AZSUNA

The old ruins of Azsuna hold the charm of a place to explore rather than memories of a city that once existed; their tragedy is not mine. The history of those ruins remains fascinating—the once-queen Azshara betrayed her people to Sargeras for power, and the spirits of those she wronged still wander the land eternally as full souls rather than confused and vengeful echoes.

I passed through the Drowned Gardens and the Crumbled Palace to appreciate their majestic ruins and imagine what words Lor'themar might weave together at the sight. With the Legion gone and Prince Farondis redeemed, the ghosts of Nar'thalas are no quieter nor more restful, though they are measurably happier. A couple of nightborne scholars have made it their work to break the curse Azshara laid; strange to think that the ruins might someday be depopulated of their spirits, but change comes to all things.

Azurewing Repose struck me as a potential location to honeymoon, with its deep-blue magic-rich pool and crystal-lined cave. It had been tranquil for a while, after its draconic residents were called to the reformation of the blue dragonflight. Knowing they no longer make their home at the Repose, I was surprised to see a number of young drakes and whelplings there, watched over by the old wardens. It seems the Repose has become something of a vacation spot for the blue dragons. It was charming to watch the whelplings play, but there was a bit too much youthful shrieking (children of all peoples seem to have that in common) for there to be any possibility of a romantic air.

NAR'THALAS ACADEMY

Of greater Nar'thalas, the academy is being rebuilt—and rightfully so! It was the center for all magical learning in its time. Ghosts still far outnumber the living, but new students are coming. I'd certainly like to spend time combing through the libraries, ragged as they still might be, and the Hall of Antiquities.

The dress code is back in place, and all students need the requisite hat and robes. I think I won't warn Lor'themar about that, should I bring him here. I will keep this in mind as a potential detour, rather than a destination.

I'm glad you forgot about this planned trick of yours when you offered to let me look through your notes!

EYE OF AZSHARA

The Eye of Azshara, despite its name, is a lovely sandy beach and wave-washed cove, perfect for swimming and laying about on the sand while reading—and with a bit of forest and caves to explore as well. While the naga have been driven off, there is still a hint of danger from the murlocs and snapping turtles. Nothing Lor'themar and I could not easily handle . . . though a nip from a hungry turtle would certainly dampen the mood.

This was truly more an opportunity to check on the Vault of the Wardens. The Watchers were . . . about as forthcoming as ever, but while they owe no allegiance to me, I did convince them I had a reasonable interest in knowing what was happening in a place filled with such dangerous prisoners. It seems they've contained the mess that transpired here years ago, by the reckoning of the Watcher I spoke with—and the wards are still holding at full power.

GARDEN OF ELUNE

The Garden of Elune had all the quiet that the Azurewing Repose lacked; the shadowfiends that once stalked the grounds have been wiped clear; the ruins are now silent and empty but for the banshees that wander them. The nearby Temple of a Thousand Lights, still pointedly towering over the garden, is even more intact—and restful as long as one sidesteps the shades of former arcanists and ignores their shouting about Azshara. Neither place is so green as the rest of Azsuna, but there's a beauty to their ruins like no other place, perhaps because of the secrets they might still hold.

I spent a bit of time poking through rubble; it's always been a place I've enjoyed exploring, though I don't think Lor'themar would find it so fascinating as I do.

Nor would I enjoy being upstaged by your romance with a crumbling wall!

THE BROKEN SHORE

Of anywhere in the Broken Isles, the Broken Shore has undergone the most profound of transformations. I remember well what the land looked like only a few years ago, during the Legion's invasion: war-scorched ground that seemed it would never grow anything again, pools of fel, roaming demons, and monstrous spiders. Now? It is no Val'sharah, but its transformation under the careful eye of druids and shaman is marked. The waters that wash the shore and run in its streams are clear. Hardy plants now cover the ground in patches of dense green dotted with flowers, and the air smells *alive* in a way I never imagined it would again. This, I would show Lor'themar, to stand with him at living proof that grave wounds may be healed.

The old base at Deliverance Point remains, though its buildings have been repurposed to more peaceful ends; the mage tower and nether disruptor have been given over to the Kirin Tor for research, while the command center itself serves as more of a dormitory for visitors and a guard contingent.

Instead, you made the mistake of letting me read this journal. Quite the tactical error, love.

It remains the greatest luck and blessing of my life, Thalyssra, that you chose to pursue me rather than allowing yourself to be alone.

TOMB OF SARGERAS

The Tomb of Sargeras still hangs over the island of Thal'dranath like a threat of annihilation given form. While the tomb no longer glows sickly from within, there is an air of darkness to it that I fear may never leave. Stones steeping for centuries in evil do not release their shadows overnight.

One could hardly fathom settling here for any length of time, though the tomb was the true purpose of my visit to the Broken Shore. It is still guarded by the Watchers, though they did not give me any trouble when it came to entering, no doubt helped by me sending a message ahead so that my arrival was expected. There was someone in the tomb I wished to speak to: Aegwynn, or rather, her echo. I had heard that her echo had become more active of late. How could I resist the chance to speak to one of the greatest intellects to ever bend arcane magic to her will?

I found Aegwynn's echo in the portion of the tomb that was once the Temple of Elune, now called the Cathedral of Eternal Night. Belying that name, it was quite bright inside, graced by a sunny day, and at first I could barely see Aegwynn's echo, she was so like the light itself. I greeted her politely, introduced myself, and then we spent the next several hours pleasantly discussing various magical techniques. (I took extensive notes in a different volume that can be arcanely locked, which I think says more than enough about what we might have discussed.)

Toward the end of our conversation, I made an idle comment, more as a joke to myself than anything else: "Good thing I came here without Lor'themar. I'd never be able to keep his nose out of his work without being called a hypocrite."

Aegwynn *laughed*, a musical crescendo that was such a departure from the previous discussion, I nearly startled. There was a definite sparkle in her eye when she asked me to tell her of my Lor'themar. The conversation we had . . . I've done my best to copy it down here:

"Sounds like you're quite taken with him."

"Yes, I'd like to keep him."

"Women like you and I, some would say we have no time to love, that our first and final love must be to those whom we protect and steward. But to love as the common folk do is to know what makes our people—and indeed this world—worth saving. It's all too easy to be alone without even trying. When we find the chance to love . . . we must seize it. Hold fast to it. Guard that love as fiercely as you guard your kind. It's the one part of yourself you must never give away."

I'd complain, but we both know I wouldn't understand even a tenth of it. Someday, I pray you will teach me Shalassian.

–II–
VAL'SHARAH

I returned to Deliverance Point still thinking of Aegwynn's words, rather bemused by them, in fact. I was already following her advice, considering the trouble I'd taken to wrest myself from Suramar to spend what precious time I could with Lor'themar. As I discussed with Illidari Calia where I planned to fly next (she had also asked me how I found the tomb), we were interrupted by the arrival of a nightborne messenger, who landed and breathlessly thrust a bit of parchment at me. Strange, to find one's heart sinking at the sight of familiar features, but there is little good news that lands so urgently.

For once, I was wrong—and never have I been gladder to be so! The message, in Thaedris's unadorned hand, began with the briefest of apologies for interrupting me, but got to the point with commendable speed (the hallmark of why I took him into my service). And what news! Lor'themar's ship had arrived! Calia, plainly amused, offered her fastest mount, and I rushed to Astravar Harbor to welcome my love. Later, once there was breath for talking, we agreed to continue journeying through the Broken Isles together.

I had already planned my next destination: as green and beautiful as I find Azsuna, Val'sharah puts it to shame. This was no surprise; it was molded to be as close to the Emerald Dream as a mortal place can be, and the druids make it their life's work to maintain this place as sacred.

Easier that way to see if there's a place we both find suitable! And far better than traveling alone.

SHALADRASSIL

The twisted crown of Shaladrassil's boughs is visible from across the Broken Isles, a bare and agonized hand reaching ever skyward. It had been a stark image when I'd staggered from Suramar's shield in the days of strife, the mockery of a horizon I had once known. I learned later that this horrifying sight spoke of the corruption the Nightmare Lord Xavius had wrought. Worse were the roots of Shaladrassil, which once anchored and protected the lands but instead grew to spread the corruption; one made it as far as the borders of Suramar before Xavius was slain and the Emerald Nightmare was purged from the tree.

The land beneath Shaladrassil has recovered and is once more verdant with life, no doubt thanks to the efforts of the druids who call Val'sharah their home. Yet the ruin of the great tree remains as an indelible reminder: there is no healing some wounds; scars will remain, and though life may return, may even be stronger than before, it will always be different.

Under the dark branches of Shaladrassil, Lor'themar and I stood quietly for a time, leaning against each other, Lor'themar's arm loose and warm about my waist as we watched the birds and butterflies and other small creatures who had returned go about their business. A place of both beauty and sorrow to spend a moment . . . but I think not a honeymoon.

Though it wouldn't hurt to spend some quiet time and celebrate life a little, eh?

DREAMGROVE

In a place that is already meant to echo the Dream, the Dreamgrove is almost . . . too much for me. It was an honor for us to see it at all, a treat that Koda Steelclaw offered us: the rare chance for non-druids to see the place where our land and the Emerald Dream meet. She also warned us not to wander far from her, as even druids may take decades to truly learn the navigation of this grove. A great many have, it seems—there were many druids present, training and meditating. Koda told us it was, too, the place where the druids planned their defense during the Legion's assault. There's much knowledge here, but very little of it is for a curious arcanist to explore.

I as well, love. The grove is meant for druids, and there's no mistaking either of us for one of those!

BRADENSBROOK

Bradensbrook is a much lighter and happier place than it once was. The little village of refugees has grown quite a bit larger, helped along by their more welcoming attitude since their encounter with Jarod Shadowsong during the Legion's invasion—and the trade they've since established with the Temple of Elune. Black Rook Hold still towers over the village like a brooding shadow, but with Lord Ravencrest and its other ghosts having been laid to rest by the efforts of both Horde and Alliance, there's little to trouble them.

Lor'themar thought a quaint village would make a quiet honeymoon stop—the inn alone looked like something out of a storybook, all well-worn wood and flower-embroidered cushions on the chairs, with a local piper playing softly in the corner to add a bit of atmosphere for all who were dining. Our entrance caused a small stir, but no one troubled us; rather, we were cheerfully greeted by an elderly gentleman, who waved us to an empty table. He introduced himself as Eliyah and continued, "Can tell you what my husband's got cookin' tonight, if you like, or I can read your fortunes and pick somethin' for you myself," he said, his eyes twinkling.

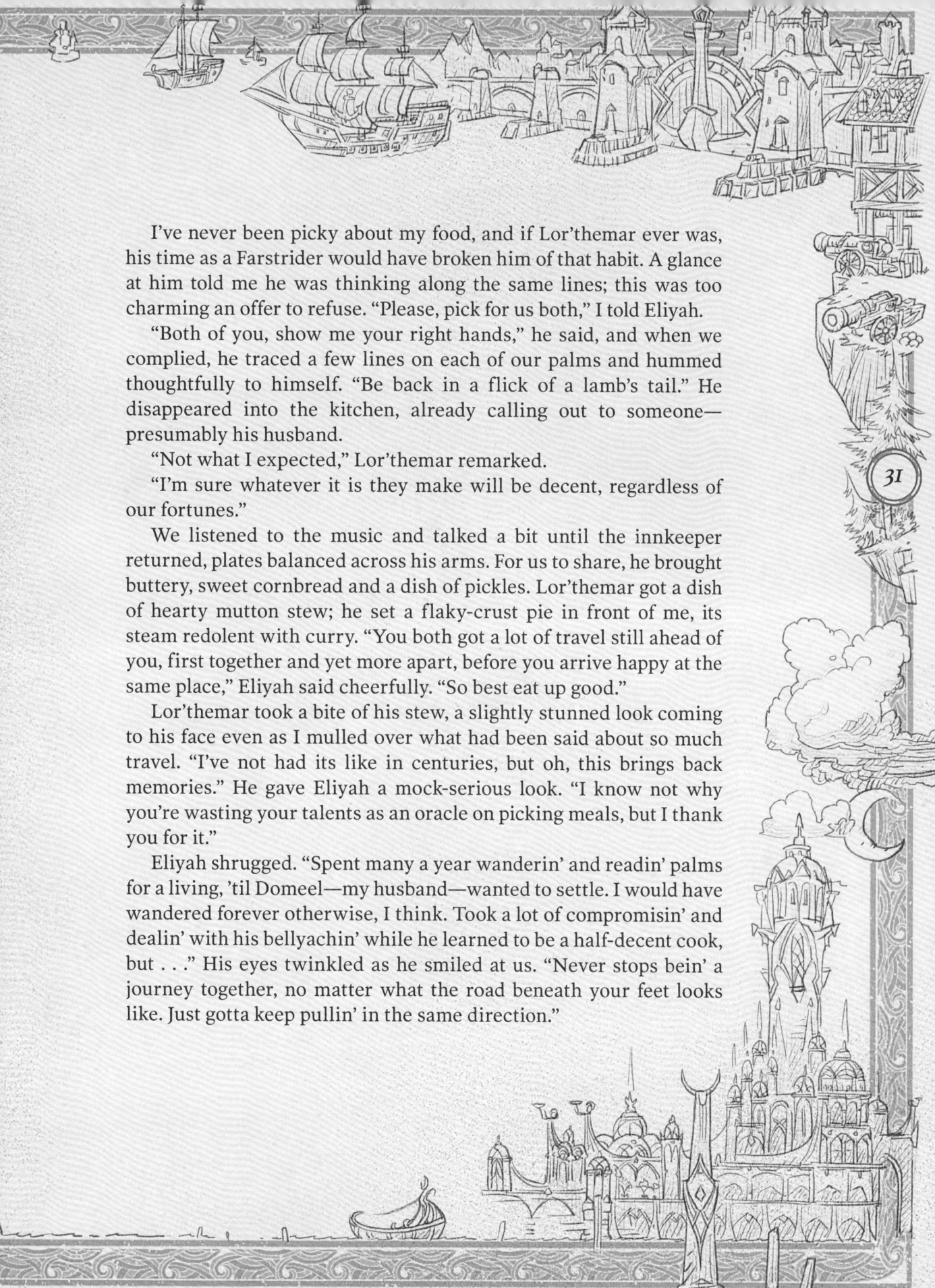

I've never been picky about my food, and if Lor'themar ever was, his time as a Farstrider would have broken him of that habit. A glance at him told me he was thinking along the same lines; this was too charming an offer to refuse. "Please, pick for us both," I told Eliyah.

"Both of you, show me your right hands," he said, and when we complied, he traced a few lines on each of our palms and hummed thoughtfully to himself. "Be back in a flick of a lamb's tail." He disappeared into the kitchen, already calling out to someone—presumably his husband.

"Not what I expected," Lor'themar remarked.

"I'm sure whatever it is they make will be decent, regardless of our fortunes."

We listened to the music and talked a bit until the innkeeper returned, plates balanced across his arms. For us to share, he brought buttery, sweet cornbread and a dish of pickles. Lor'themar got a dish of hearty mutton stew; he set a flaky-crust pie in front of me, its steam redolent with curry. "You both got a lot of travel still ahead of you, first together and yet more apart, before you arrive happy at the same place," Eliyah said cheerfully. "So best eat up good."

Lor'themar took a bite of his stew, a slightly stunned look coming to his face even as I mulled over what had been said about so much travel. "I've not had its like in centuries, but oh, this brings back memories." He gave Eliyah a mock-serious look. "I know not why you're wasting your talents as an oracle on picking meals, but I thank you for it."

Eliyah shrugged. "Spent many a year wanderin' and readin' palms for a living, 'til Domeel—my husband—wanted to settle. I would have wandered forever otherwise, I think. Took a lot of compromisin' and dealin' with his bellyachin' while he learned to be a half-decent cook, but . . ." His eyes twinkled as he smiled at us. "Never stops bein' a journey together, no matter what the road beneath your feet looks like. Just gotta keep pullin' in the same direction."

GARDEN OF THE MOON

I remember visiting the Temple of Elune as a young girl; the structure of the temple itself is ancient and unchanged, though I can see places where the stone has been chipped or cracked, where repairs have rounded what were once sharp edges, where carvings have been cleaned or updated. But there is an air to it, both of weariness and strength. The most recent invasion was not the first time the temple has withstood assault by the Legion. But this time, the temple and its adherents bore witness to the corruption and death of Ysera and saw the Tears of Elune come forth in response. Such weighty sorrow cannot help but leave its mark on any place.

I had meant to simply pass briefly through so that Lor'themar could see the temple, but I found myself sitting on one of the stone benches, regarding the temple's small moon mirror that has survived through so much. I am not generally one who prays; I've always had little patience to utter quiet words when there is action to be taken. But there was nothing to be done here except . . . remember. Lor'themar stood at my back like a shield, one hand resting on my shoulder, unmoving but for the slow, smoothing motion of his thumb as I found it in myself to pray—that this would be the last time Elune's temple would see such sorrow.

Other scars of the Legion's attack are visible if one knows where to look for them. It is plain how much new growth there is in the Garden of the Moon and in Malorne's Refuge, replacing that which was destroyed by demons and satyrs. It's the way of nature, to heal itself, and the way of elves to see scar layered on scar when we have so many years in which to observe.

And we mark our own scars as well, to find beauty in them. I do wish we had stayed at the temple longer . . .

LORLATHIL

Lorlathil looks much like any other village in Val'sharah: a place of night elves, dryads, and keepers of the grove. A home to druids, like many others. Lor'themar decided we ought to stop there after spotting their large herd of hippogryphs, and they were magnificent creatures! After watching the chicks gambol about, I snuck off to satisfy my curiosity about the more interesting fact of the village—it was the birthplace of the Stormrage twins. I hoped to find some books or stories or . . . I don't know, *something* of note. No luck there.

Time to continue on to Highmountain. The beauty of Val'sharah is without rival, but I suspect none save druids, tauren, or night elves could honeymoon here.

I think we might have found something very suitable, if we'd spent a bit more time looking—and if you'd let yourself relax. Why are you in such a rush, love?

ARMOR ASIDE: VESTMENT OF SECOND SIGHT

For all their generally dour nature and looks that have made many a nightborne recoil in fear and disgust, I hold a reluctant respect for the demon hunters. I am of course under no illusions that they joined our war in the Broken Isles out of love for the nightborne. Still, I appreciate the single-mindedness with which they meted out death to the demons that Elisande sold our people to . . . even as I condemn their use of fel magic in doing so. I find their armor in keeping with their general demeanor, dark and serious and, I suppose, quite aerodynamic for when they take flight.

HIGHMOUNTAIN

The wilds of Highmountain are perhaps a little too wild for my taste, but I knew it was a place that would speak to Lor'themar. We flew on hippogryphs borrowed from Lorlathil to better take in the rugged beauty of the mountains. This served the dual purpose of saving my feet from the blisters I could all but feel coming . . . and kept Lor'themar from making friends with every passing tree and stag.

We landed at Skyhorn, since it commands the best view of Highmountain. The harpies that once haunted its crags with their shrieks are no longer bold enough to be on the attack at the least, thanks to the tauren. It did my heart good to see the landscape once torn by war and corruption so healed. We stood for a bit in silence and enjoyed the cool breeze, but . . . I felt restless rather than content, my thoughts quickly wandering to the relations between Highmountain and Suramar.

It was sheer luck that we were interrupted by a messenger before I could spoil Lor'themar's quiet myself. Little goes on in Highmountain without Mayla knowing—good, since she is the high chieftain!—and better, we were invited to dinner.

As if I could be so distracted with you at my side.

THUNDER TOTEM

The great lodge at Thunder Totem towers over its valley from the mesa... yet still seems somehow small against the great granite backdrop of Highmountain Peak. There are more tauren here than ever, more laughter, more little ones running and playing. The Highmountain tauren have prospered much since ousting the Underking, Dargrul, and joining the Horde. Mayla greeted us warmly and swept us off to a feast large enough to feed an army, yet it still felt very cozy, just a few of us sitting around the massive spread of beautifully carved wooden bowls filled with salmon cooked in the drogbar style, salt and pepper shank, and barracuda mrglgagh—with an utter mountain of fry bread with which to eat it.

Mayla gave us the news of Highmountain—Riverbend Village had been fully rebuilt by the Rivermane, blessed by a circle of shaman one season past; Snowblind Mesa was home to a trading post of Stonedark drogbar, the wary relations between their peoples well and truly mending. It was with apparent bemusement that she told us the drogbar had been bringing tales of strange sounds coming from Neltharion's old lair, curious sighs and whispers on the air.

Ha! I knew it wasn't an accident!

"Have you heard them?" Lor'themar asked.

Mayla shrugged. "Not when I visited."

"I could—" At which point I observed the tilt of his shoulders that said he was going into official business, so I *accidentally* dropped a spiced rib on his lap.

That thread of conversation was mercifully forgotten by the time I cleaned up the mess (though I will ask Mayla about it later, when we aren't attempting a vacation), but then Mayla mentioned Horde business. Before I felt compelled to have another moment of clumsiness with a serving platter, Lor'themar had brought the topic around to his friend Baine, with an *entirely* subtle: "I miss the fellow. I've not seen him in a bit. Have you?" When Mayla admitted she'd seen Baine just last week, my love followed with an *even more subtle*: "Wonderful! He's excellent company, wouldn't you agree?"

To which Mayla—very blandly—answered: "I hadn't noticed."

Good for Baine, I say. But never let me gamble with Mayla.

TRUESHOT LODGE & SYLVAN FALLS

After a long sleep (among some very comfortable furs) to recover from the feast, we bid farewell to Mayla and headed out once again into the mountains. Lor'themar suggested we go by Sylvan Falls, a place we both recalled as having a beautiful view.

On the way there, he had his attention stolen by the path to Trueshot Lodge. It isn't a place strictly of interest to me, as a gathering point for hunters. But Lor'themar was in his element. He challenged a few of the hunters about to an impromptu archery contest and put on quite the show—though he then threw the match to them to be a good sport. That prompted him to tell stories of his time as a Farstrider, most of which I'd not heard yet myself. A very pleasant morning, all told, though I think Lor'themar might have stayed longer if I'd let him.

Sylvan Falls, far below the lodge and a bit southwest, was grander still than my memory promised. The wide stone platform built on the overlook was damp and slick with mist; a good thing both of us are fairly sure-footed. We sat together on the plinth under the statue of the archer and let a bit of time pass, Lor'themar's head on my shoulder and my cheek against the soft locks of his hair.

"This would be a lovely place for a second wedding," he remarked.

"A small one."

"Something just for us."

"I'd like a first honeymoon before a second wedding."

"We could have that here too."

The falls were lovely, yes, but . . . so close to home. To everything I must do and be. And I couldn't imagine coming back from such a trip and having no new stories to share.

"I want something new," I said. "For both of us."

I've no idea what you mean. I've hardly hefted a bow in years, and not in earnest since my days amongst the Farstriders.

> *I'll admit, I don't enjoy having every one of my suggestions summarily dismissed...*

—III—
STORMHEIM

We didn't quite argue at Sylvan Falls, but there was a tension of misunderstanding between us. We turned back toward Suramar, still with no destination in mind, but agreed to see a few sights along the way. The easiest path back lay through Stormheim. While not a place in contention for a vacation—for obvious reasons—I knew Lor'themar would enjoy having a look around as we traveled. It is certainly his sort of place, all deep, dark forests and rough-hewn mountains. (And with more than a few Titan-sourced mysteries still about to catch my curiosity as well.)

With Skovald so long dead and Sigryn the proven queen, the Tideskorn vrykul are still not what I would call friendly, but they are no longer hostile to outsiders. The kvaldir mists have been fully driven back from Tideskorn Harbor, leaving the dark waters of the Helmouth Shallows to glimmer in the thin sunlight. I was curious as to the renewed state of the rest of the land, so we continued southeast to see the Field of Fallen Kings and the canyon (or is it a quarry? I can't tell, with how much the vrykul have carved into it) they call Haustvald and hold as a holy place. Both were once places skewed by runic magics. The undead have since been laid to rest, and Haustvald seems to be once more used for religious rites that don't involve necromancy.

> *"Benignly standoffish until you've shared a few drinks" is the way I'd best describe them.*

RUNEWOOD

The way Lor'themar lit up when he spotted the golden expanse of the Runewood was a sight to behold. I think the Runewood is far more like the woods he spent his younger years in than the druid haven of Val'sharah.

It was a pleasant enough walk—and lovely to see Lor'themar truly in his element—but after an hour of looking at trees that were all fairly similar to one another, I was a bit petulant with him when he suggested we sit in a clearing. It was, in my defense, essentially the same as the last clearing he'd wanted to sun himself in.

It wasn't at all the same—but that's not the point. If we're to have a vacation, then you need to relax as well! Breathe and be in the moment . . . with me.

We'd already agreed that this wouldn't be our spot for a vacation. There wasn't anything else to do!

HRYDSHAL

I believe the actual term used was "ice-rimed arse-kicking."

As an apology for being disagreeable earlier, I suggested we stop by the vrykul city of Hrydshal. The denizens are thankfully much friendlier than they were before—and have stopped their practice of kidnapping and tormenting the local Thorignir storm drakes to "train" them. Their technique now seems to be one of much more mutual respect and learning. It was . . . not something I found personally arresting, but Lor'themar's fascination and happiness—and him volunteering for a demonstration at one point—more than made up for it. His friendliness did earn him the information that what had so profoundly changed the relationship between vrykul and Thorignir was the "intervention" of Vyranoth with Odyn himself. Thus, most of the storm drakes have returned to the Dragon Isles, and those who stayed must be treated with respect, lest they leave as well. I wonder why I hadn't heard of this development sooner . . .

Because it is interesting but not immediately relevant to the running of Suramar, I should think. You cannot be in all places at once, love.

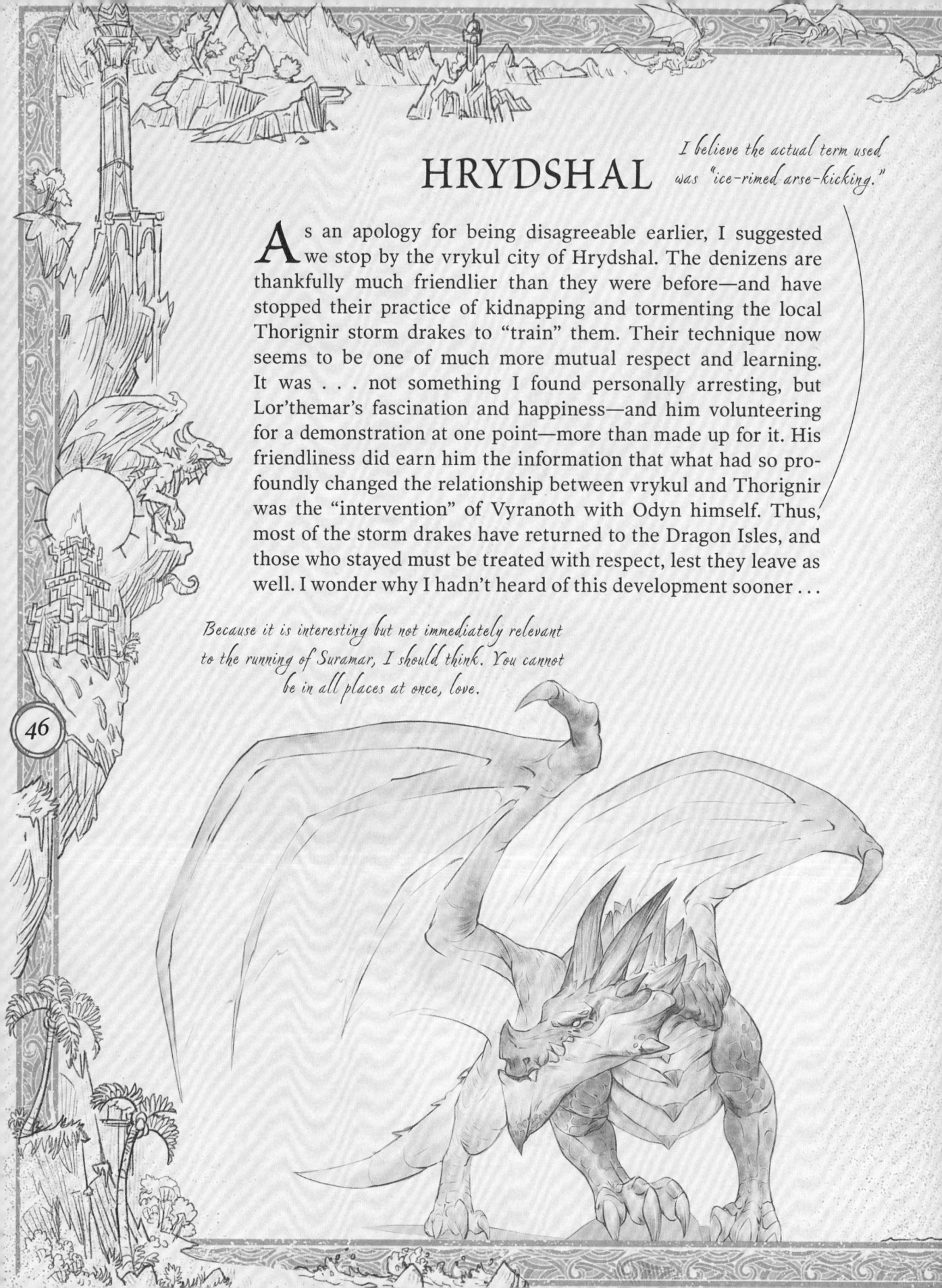

SHIELD'S REST & TOMB OF THE OLD KINGS

Compelled by stories of powerful beasts (and no more undead) from the drake tamers, Lor'themar insisted we borrow a boat to go to the island of Shield's Rest. While Lor'themar disappeared to the wilder parts of the island to stalk something with teeth large enough to take off his head with one bite—I can only assume that was his purpose in wanting to come here—I had a look at the Tomb of the Old Kings. It still shows damage from the Legion's invasion if one knows what to look for, but the well-crafted and loving repairs being done are just as evident.

None of the old kings seemed at all interested in talking to me, I suppose, because the vrykul in general don't find anyone who isn't a sword-carrying warrior terribly interesting. I contented myself with examining the various traps that had been built into the tomb, many of which were part mechanism and part magic in an interesting way. Lor'themar returned not long after I'd given up, looking very pleased with himself and carrying a large golden feather that he offered to me like a faire prize. I do love that smile of his.

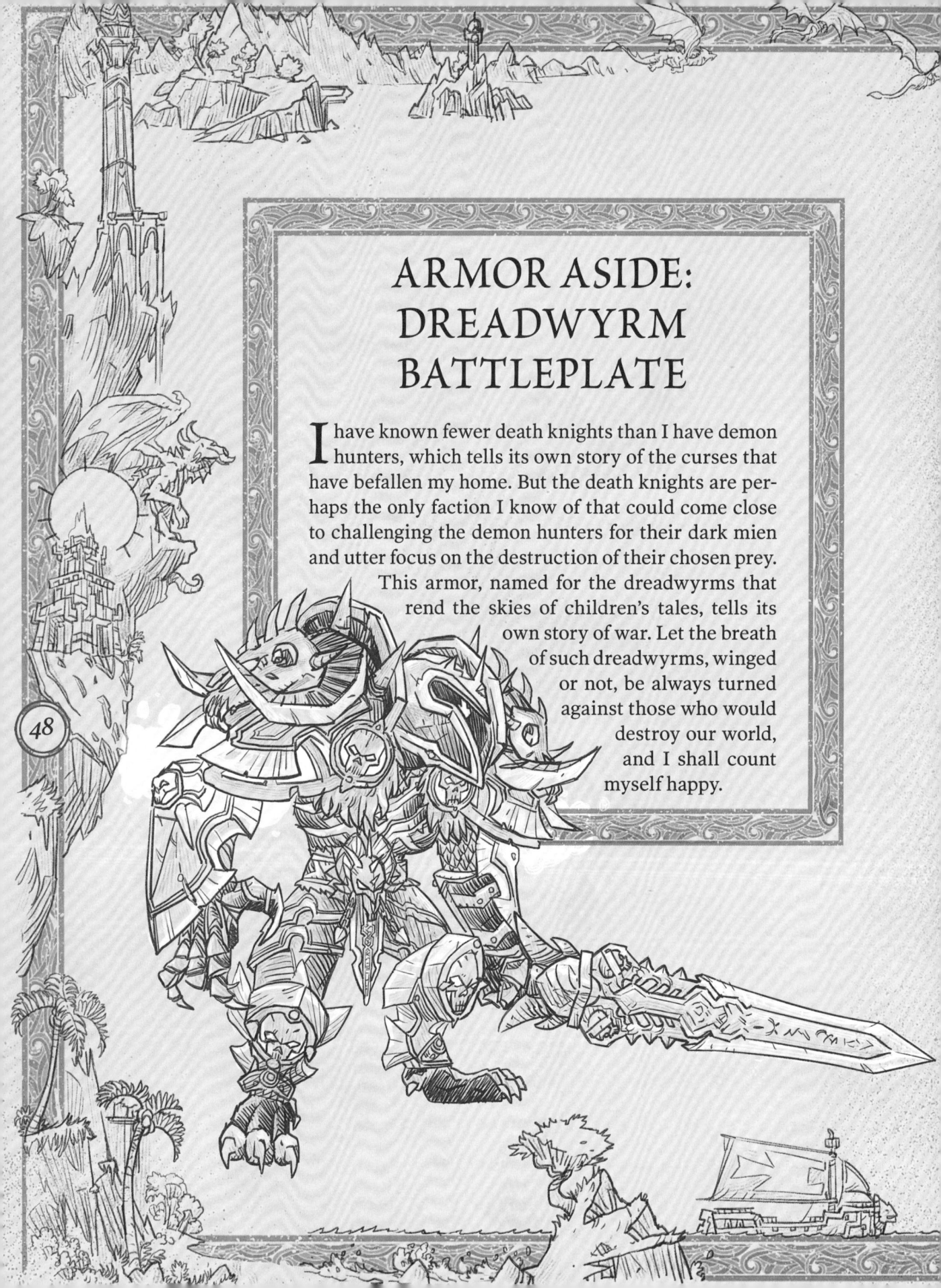

ARMOR ASIDE: DREADWYRM BATTLEPLATE

I have known fewer death knights than I have demon hunters, which tells its own story of the curses that have befallen my home. But the death knights are perhaps the only faction I know of that could come close to challenging the demon hunters for their dark mien and utter focus on the destruction of their chosen prey. This armor, named for the dreadwyrms that rend the skies of children's tales, tells its own story of war. Let the breath of such dreadwyrms, winged or not, be always turned against those who would destroy our world, and I shall count myself happy.

GATES OF VALOR & HALLS OF VALOR

While I didn't wish to keep our ship waiting, after being stymied at the Tomb of the Old Kings, I couldn't pass up the opportunity to view the Halls of Valor. Lor'themar was interested in the chance to assess the state of the vrykul's military.

While he watched the hopefuls practice, I asked one of the Val'kyr to take me to Odyn. I was informed, in a tone I did not much care for, that Odyn saw only those he deemed worthy in battle. Seeing as I had no interest in fighting our way through to him . . . I declined.

My thoughts: Impressive, but they're more likely to start a fight with each other before they'd have a go at any of us. Though I think if we offered them a chance for glorious battle, we'd have some takers.

DALARAN

Dalaran has become one of my favorite places to go, now situated in the sky here; it feels a bit like a second home to me, with the air of its wide, bright avenues filled with magic and mages of all sizes using spells so casually. I contemplated taking an airship to the city, to pass a few hours of enforced idleness, but decided I preferred to teleport us both. It felt the most fitting way to arrive at the city of mages. Lor'themar wanted to take a look at the pet shop (and stick his nose into the sewers; not my favorite place due to the ruffians that call them home, for all that they're the cleanest sewers that have ever existed), so we separated for a bit and agreed to meet back up at the Legerdemain Lounge.

SEWERS & THE VIOLET HOLD

I poked around the bookshop and picked up a lovely bottle of Zandalari wine at One More Glass before returning to the Legerdemain Lounge, only to find Lor'themar not yet there. I waited long enough to have a drink before I went looking for him. I certainly don't fear for his ability to take care of himself, but he does tend to get distracted by small things and lose track of time.

A simple spell drew me to his location . . . in the sewers. I half expected him to be exchanging bets over some sort of underground cage match, but instead I found him in an isolated corner with Khadgar, of all people. As I walked up, I heard Lor'themar say: "I saw her just before she left. Said she wanted to see her son, but after what happened at the Sunwell, I could only—"

Before Lor'themar could finish that thought, I interrupted: "Don't you dare." Khadgar looked surprised by my sudden appearance; Lor'themar had the good grace to look guilty. "We are on vacation," I added firmly, for all I had my own curiosity about such things. But they could wait; they had to. "And we are leaving, now, to enjoy our honeymoon." Lor'themar was wise enough not to argue.

Khadgar, either truly oblivious or purposefully so, simply said: "It's nothing urgent. Have a wonderful time, you two. Bring me back a souvenir."

Excuse me! I . . . quite resemble that accusation.

AEGWYNN'S GALLERY

While Lor'themar had been poking around in the city, one of the places I stopped by was Aegwynn's Gallery. While I know full well that it was a place named for the woman and I'd find no memory of her there, I wished to see what tributes to her might be there in place of the Pillars of Creation it had once held.

Instead, to my shock, I found the gallery occupied with guards and locked heavily down with wards—and the Pillars inside. When I'd gone to the Tomb of Sargeras, I had not looked for them, since the seals had seemed unstable . . . but it would take time for such instability to manifest, and this must have been a recent occurrence. That, or the Dalaran mages had found a way to ward the tomb without needing the Pillars on site.

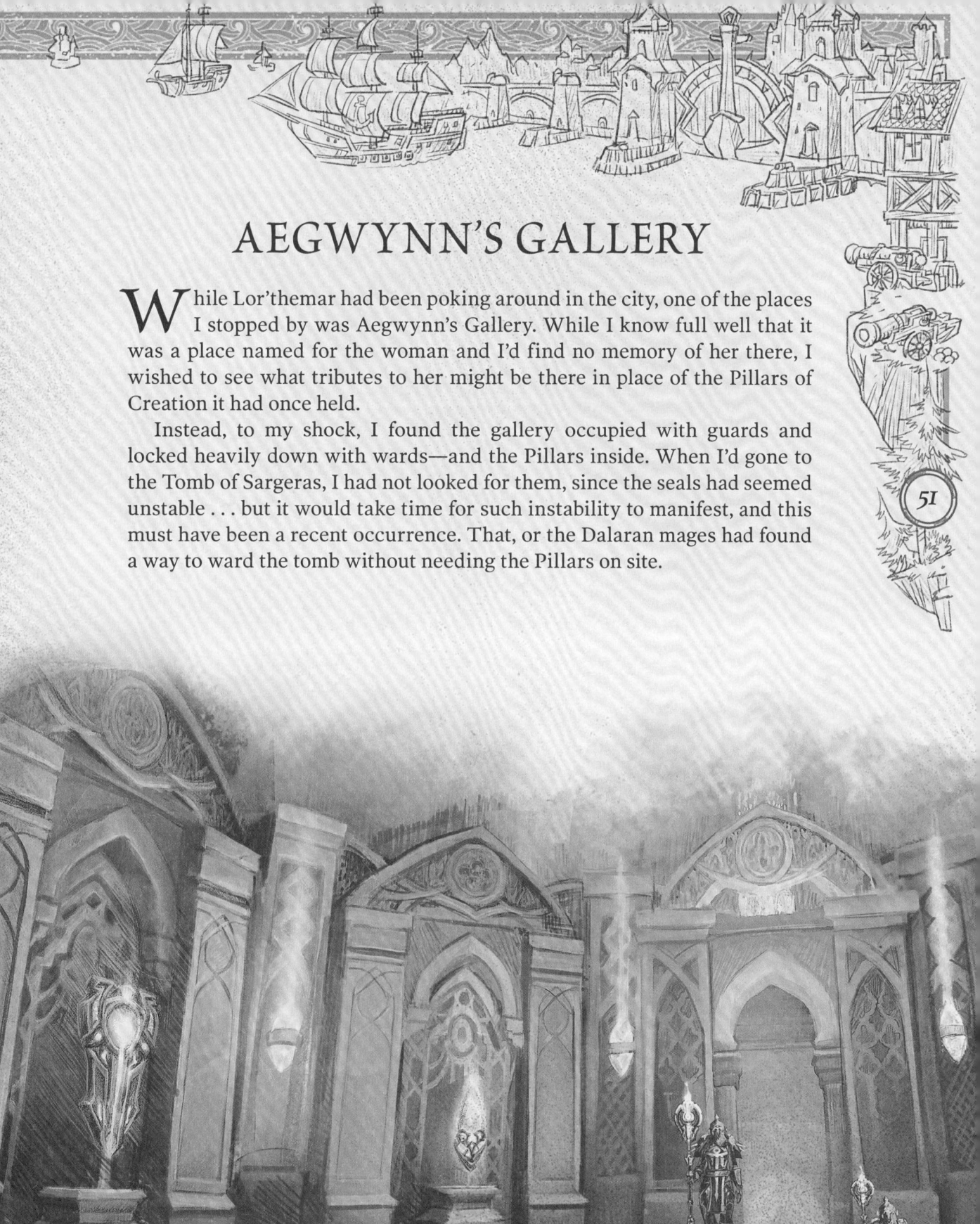

> Merely sneaking the work in behind my back, I see.
>
> Just as you were doing!

I was very tempted to ask Khadgar about this, but if Lor'themar wasn't allowed to do business, then I certainly wasn't about to mention such things in front of him. I believe that if there were something urgent that we needed to know, Khadgar would have told us.

And woe unto him if I am wrong. After I all but dragged Lor'themar away from Khadgar by the ear, he asked in a rather peevish tone: "And where is it we are going, love?"

I stopped, realizing how little good it had done so far to do this search as a pair. We seemed to alternate being annoyed with each other, in a hurry, or distracted about different things. This was not what I had wanted of what time we could carve out together, to be at odds—the opposite, in fact! I wanted to capture that romance we'd had in our stolen moments before and perfect it in time that was wholly ours. I knew better than to blame this emotional dislocation upon Lor'themar. Ten thousand years in Suramar has made me entirely too accustomed to having things my way. I needed time to untangle my own feelings before disagreement became bickering, became arguing, became . . . something worse.

> Reading this, I'm more than a little worried myself, even if I'm not up on the more arcane concerns. Khadgar will have both of us to contend with if he's been keeping trouble under his hat.

> I beg your pardon! I can be annoyed but not "peevish."

Lor'themar sensed my hesitation, I think, and offered: "A journey by ship might be best. So that is an event."

It felt like a poor idea to be in such a small space together after butting heads. It might only sharpen my temper. "There is a lot of the world to cover, even if we stay close to the Broken Isles," I offered. "We could go to two different places and look for the best location for our honeymoon."

He didn't look shocked or upset at the suggestion and told me that he had similar feelings. "Divide and conquer. An excellent idea."

We decided I would journey out to Zandalar and he to Kul Tiras. Our course thus set, we returned to Suramar to have a ship for each of us provisioned—and spend a last night together before this new parting of ways. Knowing that we'd be separated again soon, however voluntarily, certainly helped us focus on each other.

Astute as ever. I had found myself wondering if perhaps we'd spent so much time even since our wedding apart that . . . perhaps we were a bit out of step. On the other hand, we are both leaders, both used to deciding the course of so much around us. But I'd much rather relax at your side than persist in a frustrated search for I know not what.

I know not what myself. And perhaps that is the problem.

⇝ ZANDALAR ⇜

While my first arrival in Zandalar had seen me go directly from battle with the Alliance to a political viper's pit the likes of which I'd not experienced since Elisande's defeat, I still have many fond memories. By the time I saw the mist-shrouded shores, I'd had enough time on the ship to quiet my inner turmoil and refocus on what I felt was the most important. I'd made a list of places I wished to view and written a letter to be sent ahead to Queen Talanji. While Zandalar is friendly to the Horde and Talanji honored Lor'themar and me by attending our wedding, I didn't want to start off on the wrong foot by assuming my welcome.

–IV–
ZULDAZAR

I could think of no other place to begin my journey through Zandalar than the capital city of Zuldazar. Tropical warmth, colorful architecture, air scented with flowers and rain . . . it is a place perfect for any vacation, but particularly the sort that would ideally involve lounging about while wearing very little. It is also home to the palace of Dazar'alor, which remains a breathtaking sight on approach, no matter how many times I see it. The jungle rises around the city like its own roiling green ocean, the great pyramid of the temples surging above it like an island in the sky. Even as a daughter of Suramar, I cannot help but feel the weight of its ancient history.

I approve of this idea.

PORT OF ZANDALAR

In many ways, a port is a port, whether that of Suramar or Zandalar. But while my home city is recovering quickly from her isolation, there is still a sameness to the port. It is mostly nightborne ships and merchants. Zandalar has a delightful kaleidoscopic chaos to its harbor, a merry clash of languages and cultures that fill the air with the sound of hundreds of lilting accents and the warring aromas of many different cuisines.

One of Talanji's guards was waiting at the dock for my ship, a young troll woman who introduced herself as Nazara. She said she had been sent to be my guide, which I politely refused. While I am more mage than warrior, I am confident in my ability to keep my pockets unpicked and my skin in one piece. I gently sent Nazara back to Talanji with a message that I would be at the palace in time for the evening meal and I'd tender my formal greetings then. I expected Nazara to argue with me on that point, but there was a certain humor in the way she bowed in response with a murmured, "I see why she likes you."

It was still a long time until supper, so I went to Spirits Be With You for seared simmerfin and a mojo'ito. I'd been to this inn before, and it hadn't changed one bit, in the most charming way. Lor'themar would prefer their riverbeast stew, I think.

Refreshed, I walked over to the Old Seawall, with its beautiful view of the waterfalls, and then passed through the Farraki and Amani troll enclaves, which are now much friendlier places than during my first visit, when the trolls of those tribes were engaged in harassing merchants. I bypassed the Dive Bar as, like the sewers of Dalaran, a place that would be more of interest to Lor'themar than myself. I had a different destination in mind to round out my afternoon.

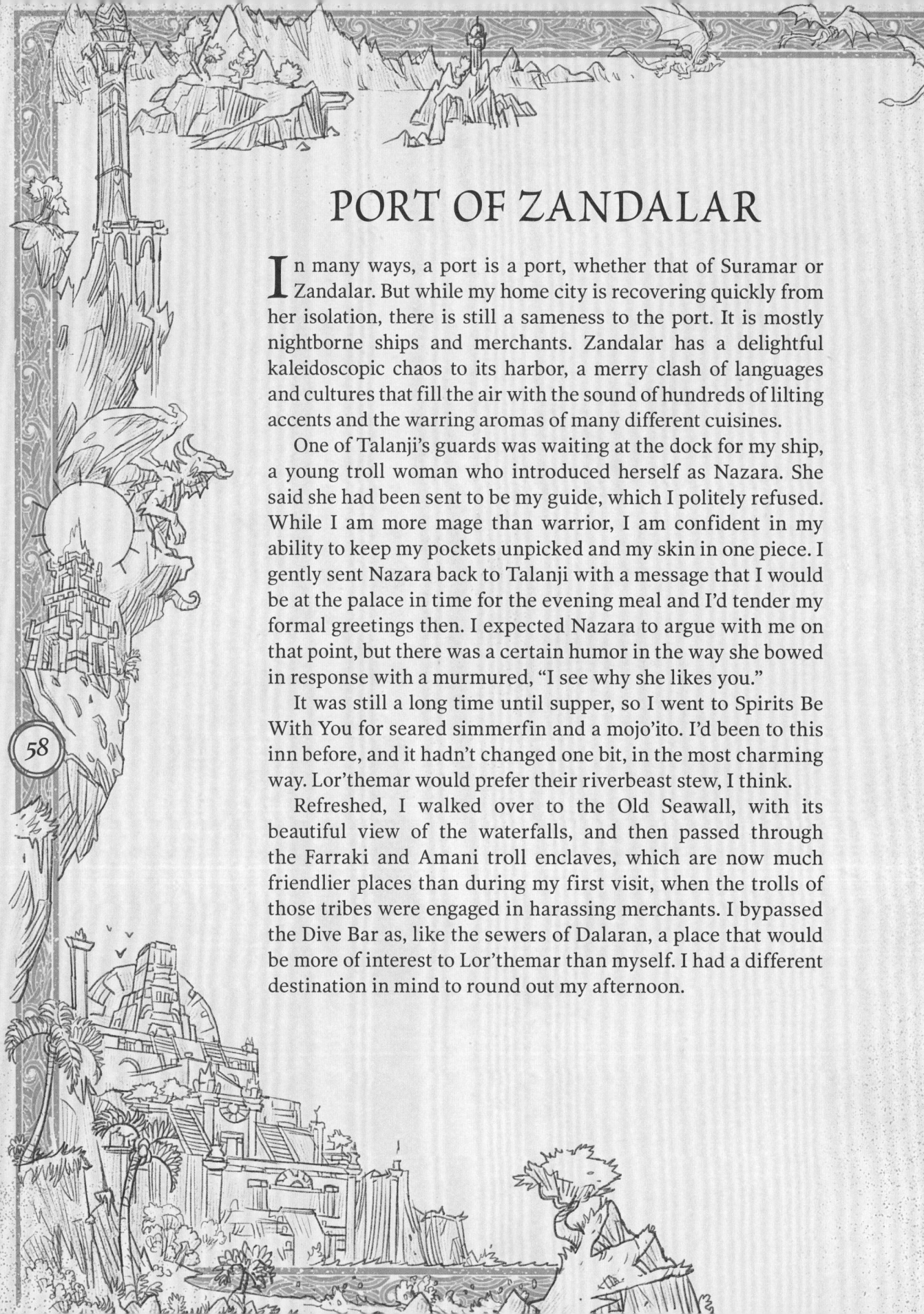

TORTOLLANS

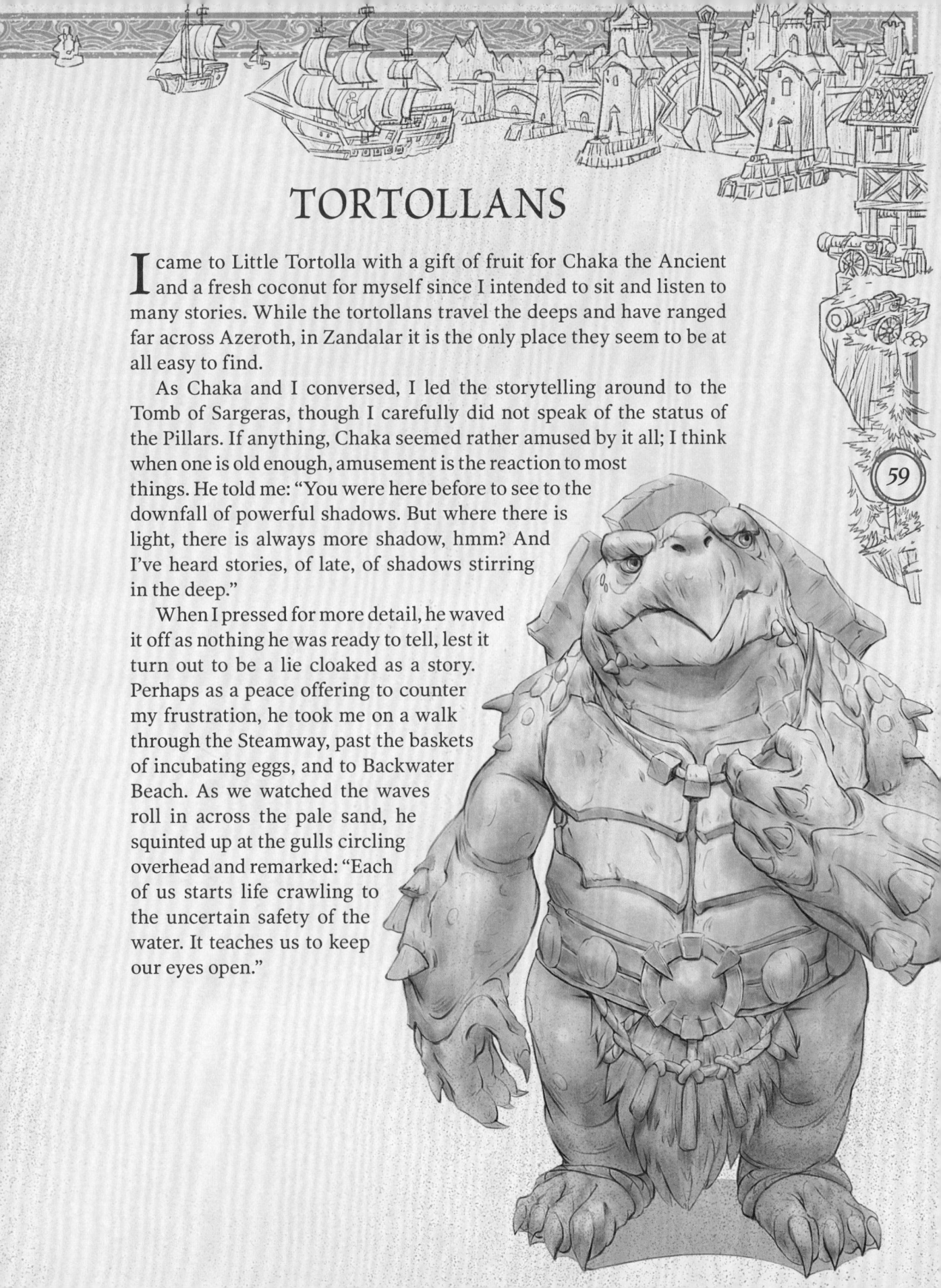

I came to Little Tortolla with a gift of fruit for Chaka the Ancient and a fresh coconut for myself since I intended to sit and listen to many stories. While the tortollans travel the deeps and have ranged far across Azeroth, in Zandalar it is the only place they seem to be at all easy to find.

As Chaka and I conversed, I led the storytelling around to the Tomb of Sargeras, though I carefully did not speak of the status of the Pillars. If anything, Chaka seemed rather amused by it all; I think when one is old enough, amusement is the reaction to most things. He told me: "You were here before to see to the downfall of powerful shadows. But where there is light, there is always more shadow, hmm? And I've heard stories, of late, of shadows stirring in the deep."

When I pressed for more detail, he waved it off as nothing he was ready to tell, lest it turn out to be a lie cloaked as a story. Perhaps as a peace offering to counter my frustration, he took me on a walk through the Steamway, past the baskets of incubating eggs, and to Backwater Beach. As we watched the waves roll in across the pale sand, he squinted up at the gulls circling overhead and remarked: "Each of us starts life crawling to the uncertain safety of the water. It teaches us to keep our eyes open."

ZANCHUL, TERRACE OF THE CHOSEN, & THE ZOCALO

The Terrace of the Speakers is still where the lesser tribes of trolls gather—and in great numbers, these days, with trade thriving thanks to peace. The Terrace of the Chosen was not quieter, as such, but had the air of all temples, some energy that hangs heavily like incense. I was... both surprised and not to see that the Chamber of Rezan still bears his name, though it is occupied solely by the loa Pa'ku now. Rezan's iconography remains, lovingly tended by former adherents, and the tale of Zul and Yazma's betrayal of the Loa of Kings has been transcribed on the stone for all to read.

The Zocalo is just as full of life and noise as the Grand Bazaar, but there is a different tone to it. The Grand Bazaar is the place for foreigners; the Zocalo is the territory of local merchants. I bought one of the Hot House's (in)famous tiki drinks and sat awhile to simply watch people pass by in the street, haggling and bickering and laughing. I think Lor'themar would be proud of me for sitting in one place so long without a book in my hand.

I am! I wish I had been there to enjoy that with you.

DAZAR'ALOR

At the appropriate hour for dinner, I finally took myself to the heart of Dazar'alor: the great pyramid. Even now, it takes my breath away; it's easily taller and covers far more ground area than any single building in Suramar. I was grateful to be offered a ride up to the top on a trained pterrordax rather than facing the daunting task of either climbing all those stairs or calculating the correct teleportation with the various magical currents wreathing the structure.

Rather than take me to the very top to see Talanji in grandeur upon the Golden Throne (though we did fly by that level; I think the rider was teasing me a bit), they instead took me to the more familiar tier of the Great Seal. Though no longer the embassy for the Horde, the portals remain from when Oculeth and I set them up years ago.

Dinner was a small affair, though as opulent in its offerings as anyone could imagine. It was plain that Talanji wanted to have space in which to speak candidly—and that we did as soon as the formalities were taken care of. We talked a bit of our respective cities, but she was far more interested in taking a moment to gossip like we were any two people meeting over wine and roasted ribs. When I told her of my purpose for visiting, she smiled broadly, a twinkle coming to her eye. "I have some ideas for such a romantic location."

"Ones you've used?" I asked.

"Bah. Reading tales of romance is more interesting than indulging in love myself."

I mentioned that I'd thought there might be something between her and Zekhan, after I saw the two together at our wedding.

She laughed. "He is a fine figure of a troll, and easy on the eyes. A good thing, too, since he's got no talk in him but of work."

I made a mental note to mention this to Lor'themar soon. Zekhan is also the sort, I think, to seem very bold because of his triumphs during the Fourth War, though he is deeply shy in many other respects.

Talanji gave me another of those smiles. "Your luck that you caught the only blood elf with enough charm to be more interesting than ruling an empire. So, let's find you a place to celebrate your fortune."

I see my friend has picked up my worst habits.

GARDEN OF THE LOA

Flying on her personal pterrordax, we went to one of Talanji's suggested locations after dinner: the Garden of the Loa. Evening had cooled the heat of the jungle to a manageable level, and we were both a bit wine-tipsy, lightly bumping our shoulders as she showed me around.

In many ways the garden is the same as it has been for thousands of years, some buildings left to be slowly retaken by the jungle. But Talanji's dedication to the equal importance of all Zandalar's loa shows in ways both subtle and vital. While she is bound first to Bwonsamdi, his place in the garden is no greater than that of the other loa—a thing she says he bellyaches about regularly despite contentedly agreeing to it not so many years ago.

It struck me, walking through the garden and seeing the colorful—and very spiky—manifestation of the loa Torcali addressing a worshipper, that the trolls' loa are what we would call wild gods. Our ways of interacting with them are different, dictated by our cultures, but they are still a manifestation of the natural world and our bond to it. Beneath the veneer of tradition, I daresay many of our beliefs are much the same.

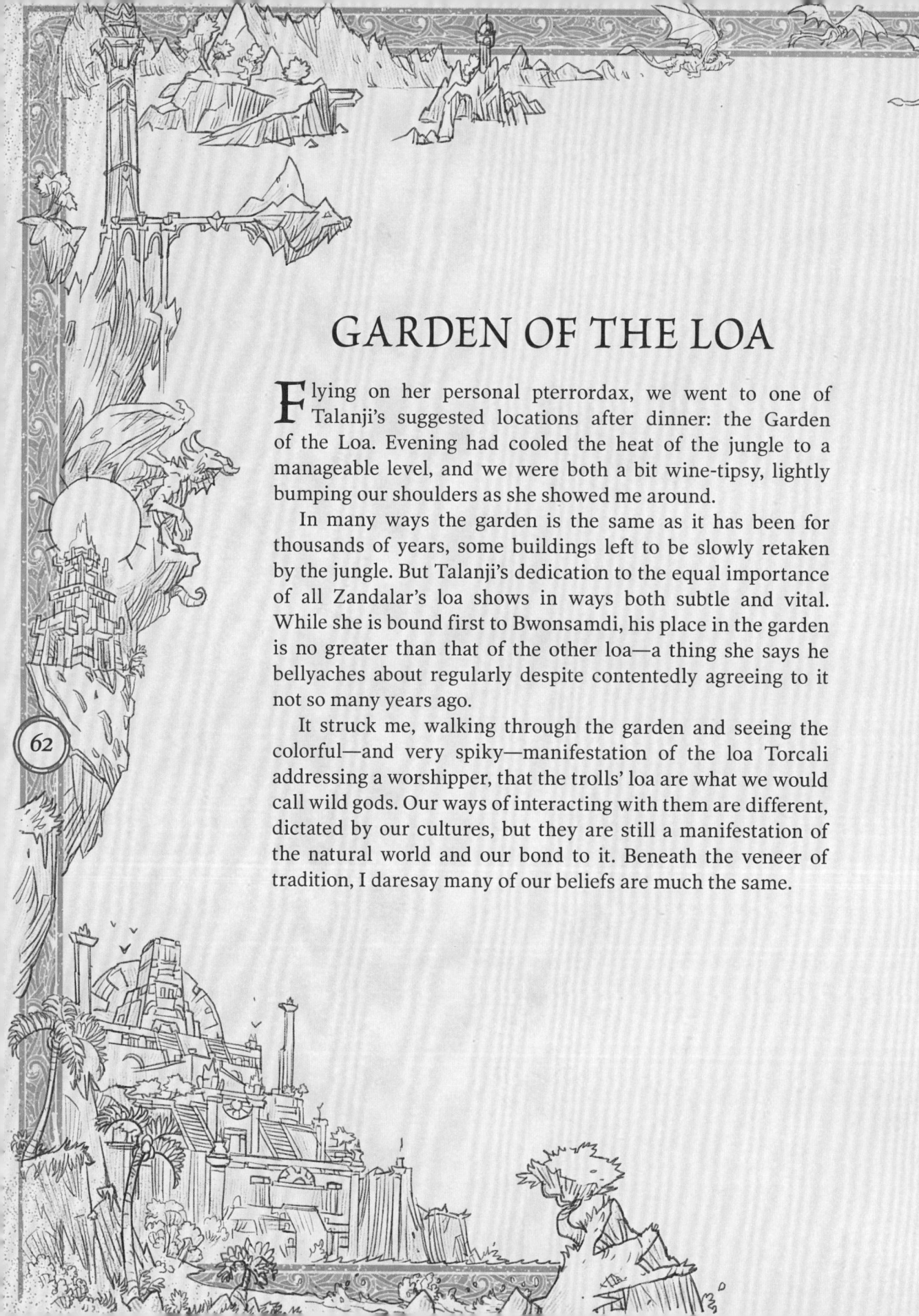

ATAL'DAZAR

I slept off my head full of wine and traveled to Atal'Dazar in the bright of the morning. Talanji could not accompany me but sent Nazara again to ease my passage through Zuldazar... without trying to guide me as such.

Much restoration has occurred in Atal'Dazar's complex of temples and now-unused palaces, to clear them of the stench of the traitors Zul and Yazma. There was a memorial there too, to commemorate where Rezan had fallen and to honor those of the Horde who then laid his tormented spirit fully to rest.

Since falling from favor long ago as a central palace, Atal'Dazar has become home to quite a few animals—Nazara said the story she believed of their origins was that they were escapees of an old royal menagerie. Handlers keep the little saurid and large skyscreamers well fed and not of a mood to try eating visitors. It didn't strike me as a restful place for a honeymoon, but nonetheless I wished that Lor'themar were with me, since he would have enjoyed the animals quite a bit... and no doubt entertained himself by teasing the clever little saurid. I drew some sketches for him, at least, to go with my next missive. I am no great artist, but I hope he will at least find them amusing.

I had quite a chuckle, I won't lie to you. I should have challenged you to a drawing contest rather than a battle of verse all those years ago.

WARBEAST KRAAL

If the beasts in Atal'Dazar made me think of Lor'themar, the Warbeast Kraal felt like a place made entirely for him. This was a true training ground for such an array of Zandalari beasts—their warhaulers and brutosaurs and so many more, shaking the very ground with their footsteps. I think he'd like the ravasaurs best, those clever little cousins of the devilsaur.

TEMPLE OF REZAN

The sprawling Temple of Rezan is hidden in the jungle northeast of the Kraal, fitting for a devilsaur loa, as something massive that somehow hide itself with ease. It seems to serve now more as a memorial to both Rezan and Rastakhan—and the priests who tend to it still use Rezan as a paragon of strength. They're careful, too, to tell the story of how Rezan was almost drained in his own temple until trolls of Zandalar and adventurers from the Horde freed him so he could rage fully upon the traitors and their mogu allies. Rezan only fell when his rage took him too far and he was separated from his fellow warriors at Atal'Dazar. It's a pointed story, and no doubt a useful one for Talanji as she tries to hold her alliances together.

XIBALA

A short journey from Rezan's Temple lie the massive bones of the first devilsaur, Xibala, preserved forever in weathered rock. Lor'themar would have delighted in all these bones larger than himself, imagining the creature they once comprised.

> *If the bones have survived this long, they'll survive for us to take a trip out to Zandalar together. Since I am rightly assuming you don't wish to have a romantic interlude amongst ancient bones . . .*

GOLDEN ROAD & TEMPLE OF THE PROPHET

Nazara suggested that, before I depart Zuldazar, I travel up the Golden Road, since it had one of the best views of the whole valley. We started at what was once the Temple of the Prophet. I expected it to have been utterly razed, considering Zul's betrayal of the Zandalari Empire. But instead, it had been replaced with a plant nursery, row after row of cultivated flowers and small fruit trees waiting to be planted. A small placard on the nursery's shop explained that much of the old stone had been taken to Pandaria, as contrition for the damage Zul had done there during his invasion, when he raised the Thunder King from death and threatened all Pandaria. Behind the shop, I found an unexpected treat—a pandaren-style garden with carefully arranged rocks and raked gravel, stalks of bamboo and bright Zandalari flowers sharing space. A small sign proudly noted that the garden had been a gift from Zouchin Village . . . and that the garden's sister plot resided near Stormstout Brewery there.

The view from the Golden Road was, indeed, breathtaking, the jungle stretching out like an ocean made of trees. One of the best views was from the Mugamba Overlook, which had once been an Alliance encampment, since peacefully ceded back to the Zandalari. The jungle has entirely erased any sign that the overlook was once occupied in war.

TAL'GURUB

Tal'gurub was also visible from the overlook, and I noted (with the help of a Far Sight spell) that it was something of a hive of troll activity. Nazara explained that Tal'gurub had been a Gurubashi enclave for a long time . . . and then one of the traitor Zul's pupils, Vol'jamba, had taken it over and slaughtered and captured its people. That was a large part of why the Gurubashi had been harassing merchants in the Great Bazaar when the Horde had first arrived; they had been a displaced population. With Tal'gurub cleansed of Vol'jamba and his followers, it was given back to the Gurubashi survivors.

ARMOR ASIDE: GRAVELORD'S DIREPLATE

It is hard, hearing of a fallen ruler, to not look to one's own experiences for context. Such is the nature of us all, I think. The stories of King Rastakhan put me in mind, at times, of Prince Farondis, making fatal mistake after fatal mistake by listening to ill advisors and not addressing the danger in his own house until it was too late.

I am proud of the part the Horde played in helping Zandalar survive traitors from within and foul magic from without. The armor made to commemorate the Battle of Dazar'alor looks as if it is made of bone, glowing with pale fire from within—fitting for warriors whose rage burns with the white-hot ferocity of the sun.

VOL'DUN

While Nazmir was visible from the Golden Road, I chose to go to Vol'dun first. I was starting to feel a bit . . . soggy. The years between my first visit to Zandalar and now—and perhaps the different season of my arrival—had left me unprepared for the constant heat and humidity. Vol'dun is certainly not *cool* by any stretch of the imagination, but at least it is a dry heat . . . and that does make a difference.

From the air, Vol'dun looks like a different sort of ocean, wave after wave of sand interrupted by near-blinding salt flats, and more ruins than whole buildings. It is breathtaking in its desolation. They say this land was once a jungle as verdant as Zuldazar until it was invaded by the C'Thraxxi warbringer Mythrax.

TEMPLE OF KIMBUL

Vol'dun's north shore is one of the few places in the region that retains—or has grown back—some of its greenery. The proximity of the ocean and the great river delta of Nazmir are one such reason . . . but the coastal mountains also sheltered it from Mythrax's destruction, centered on the old temple of Atul'Aman.

The temple to the loa Eraka no Kimbul sits on the far north of that coast, half-overgrown with trees, though there is a gentle sort of order that shows tending by caring hands. A tortollan tribe, the Tortaka, have made the temple their home and built a village at its feet. After being freed from the naga themselves, the Tortaka took Kimbul as their loa—and they have accepted non-tortollans into their ranks. There were several trolls living amongst the Tortaka, and even two sethrak.

When I asked if I might see the inside of Kimbul's temple, they were happy to extend that invitation—and as I looked over its carvings, I soon felt myself being stalked by the loa, who let out a half growl, half purr when I looked directly at him. "More attentive than most, to feel my eyes upon you," he said. I accepted the compliment, then made bold to continue the conversation. Kimbul is not a loa of magic, I quickly learned, but a loa whose wit is as sharp as his claws, and our conversation quickly became a contest of riddles that he seemed to find amusing. Oh, I wish Lor'themar had been with me for this! I held my own, but there's a reason I challenged him to poetry and not riddles.

I blame my Farstrider days. There's little else to do on long patrols once you've run out of books to read at night.

TERRACE OF THE FANG

The Terrace of the Fang is technically part of Kimbul's temple, but the tortollans have allowed it to return partially to the jungle. They have, at least, cleared it of the giant jungle spiders that once used it as a nest. As I passed by, I took note of a crew of young tortollans and trolls hunting through the ruins with torches, looking for spiderwebs to burn before more eggs could be laid. There is a small building with a clear, well-worn path to it; there, a small statue of Kimbul rests, and the tablets that record the loa's teachings.

TEMPLE OF SETHRALISS

A short journey over the coastal mountains took me to the sprawling complex surrounding the Temple of Sethraliss. Once this place was being desecrated by the sethrak faction called "the Faithless," its patron deity subdued and prevented from being reborn into the world. Thankfully, those faithful to Sethraliss have regained control of the temple and its grounds. The sethrak of the temple welcomed me, surprised to have a foreign visitor come in so boldly, as their people do still have a certain reputation because of the Faithless. Though it's been years now since war divided the sethrak, an undercurrent of mourning and exhaustion persists. I recognized their feelings all too easily.

Over cups of chilled mint tea and a shaded shelter from the hot part of the day, the temple leaders told me of their rebuilding of Sethraliss's temple. They have been slowly fostering relations with the vulpera (I saw a few trotting about the Thundering Terrace), and more recently, they contacted the Temple of Akunda. The Loa of New Beginnings has gained worshipers among the sethrak who felt too wounded by their war against the Faithless—and some of the Faithless who had laid down their arms and wished to find peace. I will admit, there are some memories in my long life—and from my own nation's civil war—I would prefer to forget . . . but I can also appreciate how I have grown from such pain. Still, I cannot fault these sethrak for forgetting. What good is learning from pain if one dies by the wound?

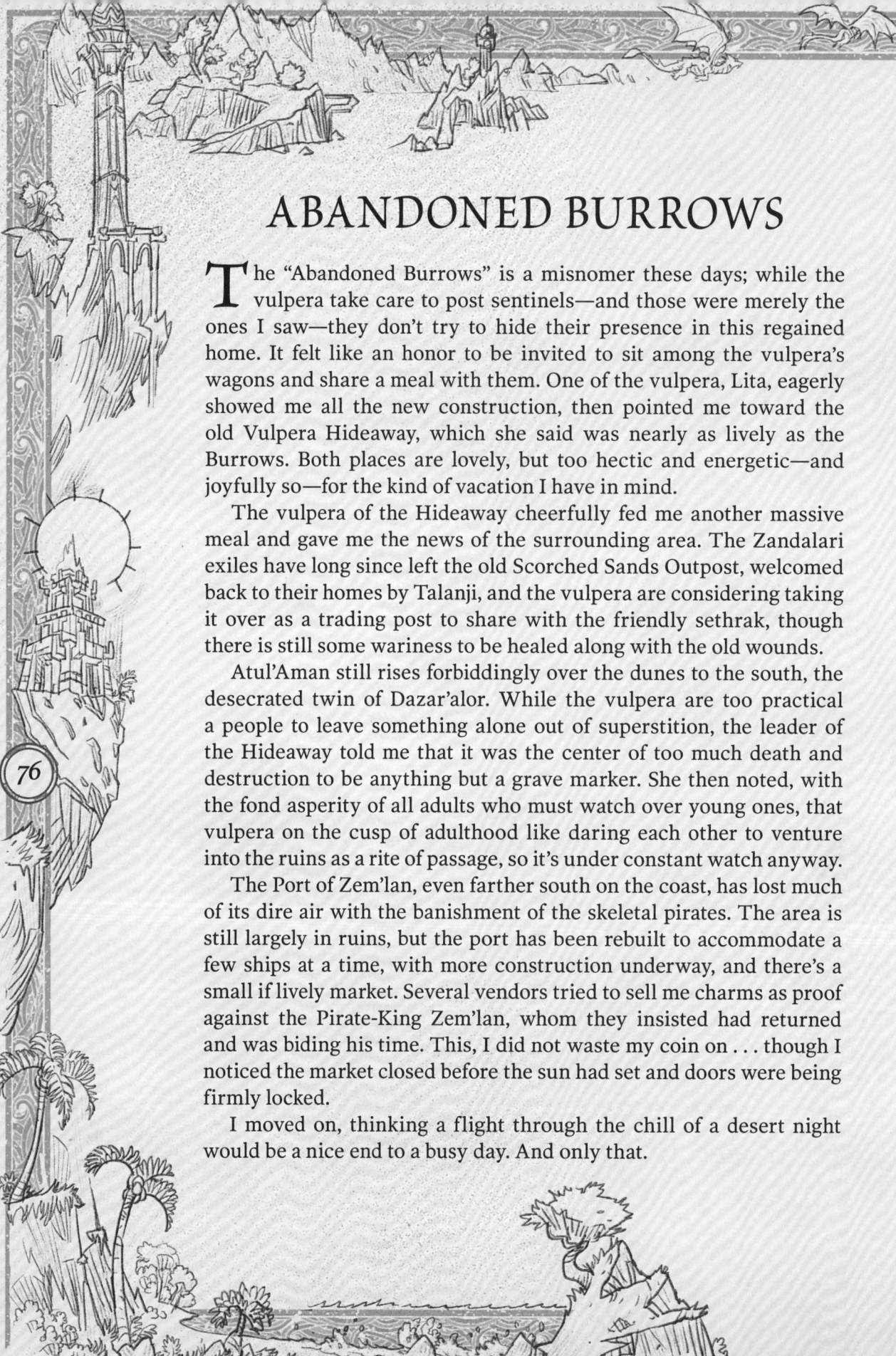

ABANDONED BURROWS

The "Abandoned Burrows" is a misnomer these days; while the vulpera take care to post sentinels—and those were merely the ones I saw—they don't try to hide their presence in this regained home. It felt like an honor to be invited to sit among the vulpera's wagons and share a meal with them. One of the vulpera, Lita, eagerly showed me all the new construction, then pointed me toward the old Vulpera Hideaway, which she said was nearly as lively as the Burrows. Both places are lovely, but too hectic and energetic—and joyfully so—for the kind of vacation I have in mind.

The vulpera of the Hideaway cheerfully fed me another massive meal and gave me the news of the surrounding area. The Zandalari exiles have long since left the old Scorched Sands Outpost, welcomed back to their homes by Talanji, and the vulpera are considering taking it over as a trading post to share with the friendly sethrak, though there is still some wariness to be healed along with the old wounds.

Atul'Aman still rises forbiddingly over the dunes to the south, the desecrated twin of Dazar'alor. While the vulpera are too practical a people to leave something alone out of superstition, the leader of the Hideaway told me that it was the center of too much death and destruction to be anything but a grave marker. She then noted, with the fond asperity of all adults who must watch over young ones, that vulpera on the cusp of adulthood like daring each other to venture into the ruins as a rite of passage, so it's under constant watch anyway.

The Port of Zem'lan, even farther south on the coast, has lost much of its dire air with the banishment of the skeletal pirates. The area is still largely in ruins, but the port has been rebuilt to accommodate a few ships at a time, with more construction underway, and there's a small if lively market. Several vendors tried to sell me charms as proof against the Pirate-King Zem'lan, whom they insisted had returned and was biding his time. This, I did not waste my coin on . . . though I noticed the market closed before the sun had set and doors were being firmly locked.

I moved on, thinking a flight through the chill of a desert night would be a nice end to a busy day. And only that.

GOLDTUSK INN

I paused for the night at the Whistlebloom Oasis, the only green place clinging to the interior of Vol'dun—and even it is quite sandy. The vulpera had mentioned the Goldtusk Inn, so I knew I wouldn't need to camp among the wasps and scorpions. I hadn't known what to expect other than a comfortable bed and, supposedly, "the best breakfast buffet this side of the Grand Bazaar." The bed was, well, not quite so much a bed as bedding and a spot in the shelter of the cavern. The breakfast buffet was less disappointing, well stocked with fresh fruit and scorpid breakfast kebabs. The place was a strange one to be sure, made all the more curious because there only seemed to be one person on staff—the proprietor himself, Rhan'ka—and rather a disquieting number of skulls, even for a troll. Rhan'ka spoke with all of them constantly, as if he was ordering them about. I gently demurred on the many "adventure packages" on offer, since I was already on an adventure of my own, and took my leave before I could be tempted into another run at the buffet.

A place Lor'themar would enjoy, if only so he could unravel its many mysteries. Too many skulls for a honeymoon, though.

Ghosts, perhaps?

I would have thought so, but there were none to be seen. Rhan'ka certainly didn't feel like a priest or a warlock, let alone one with the power to hide an entire spectral hotel staff.

I've heard living alone too long in the desert can do odd things to a person . . .

–V–
NAZMIR

After the bone-dry heat of Vol'dun, flying into Nazmir felt like running face-first into damp cloth. There is a different quality to the air in Nazmir compared to Zuldazar, a sense of decay, an undercurrent of rot that can sometimes be smelled but is felt more in the nose and mouth when one breathes.

Talanji had told me that the blood trolls were cleared from Nazmir, so the region is no longer a refuge for the corrupt practice of blood magic. But a swamp is still a swamp, a place of death and ending, and I understood why it was the territory of Bwonsamdi before I took even my first mud-soaked step.

THE NECROPOLIS

The Necropolis is the center of Bwonsamdi's power, for all that he has built new shrines in Zuldazar. His temple complex is as close to a center of power as Nazmir now has. Broken walls and fallen towers are all that remains of the old Zandalari Empire before it was driven to Zuldazar between the depredations of G'huun's minions and the ravages of time in such an environment.

While there has been enough restoration to remove the foul touch of the blood trolls, little else has been done to change its face. There is *something* about the Necropolis that set me on edge. I found myself disquieted as I stood in its great central plaza, the Court of Spirits. It was clean as such a place in a swamp could be, and quiet, yet . . . filled with whispers and living darkness even during the day. The feeling became even more unsettling within the temple, as I looked out into the darkness past the loa's altar. It was not empty . . . that, I would have found less chilling. If this is what it means to walk in the shadow of Bwonsamdi, well, I am far more impressed by Talanji's strength. No such darkness touches her.

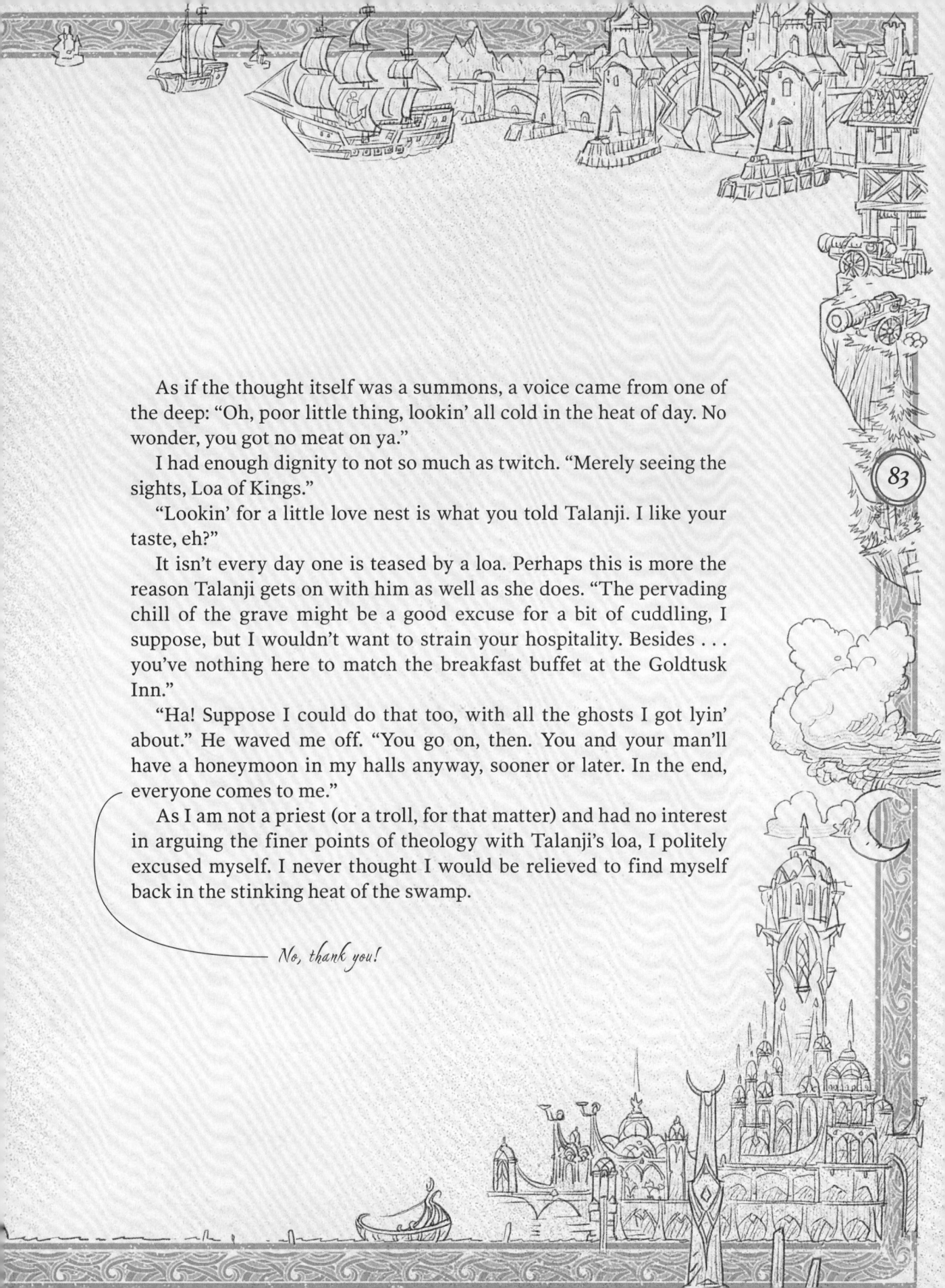

As if the thought itself was a summons, a voice came from one of the deep: "Oh, poor little thing, lookin' all cold in the heat of day. No wonder, you got no meat on ya."

I had enough dignity to not so much as twitch. "Merely seeing the sights, Loa of Kings."

"Lookin' for a little love nest is what you told Talanji. I like your taste, eh?"

It isn't every day one is teased by a loa. Perhaps this is more the reason Talanji gets on with him as well as she does. "The pervading chill of the grave might be a good excuse for a bit of cuddling, I suppose, but I wouldn't want to strain your hospitality. Besides . . . you've nothing here to match the breakfast buffet at the Goldtusk Inn."

"Ha! Suppose I could do that too, with all the ghosts I got lyin' about." He waved me off. "You go on, then. You and your man'll have a honeymoon in my halls anyway, sooner or later. In the end, everyone comes to me."

As I am not a priest (or a troll, for that matter) and had no interest in arguing the finer points of theology with Talanji's loa, I politely excused myself. I never thought I would be relieved to find myself back in the stinking heat of the swamp.

— *No, thank you!*

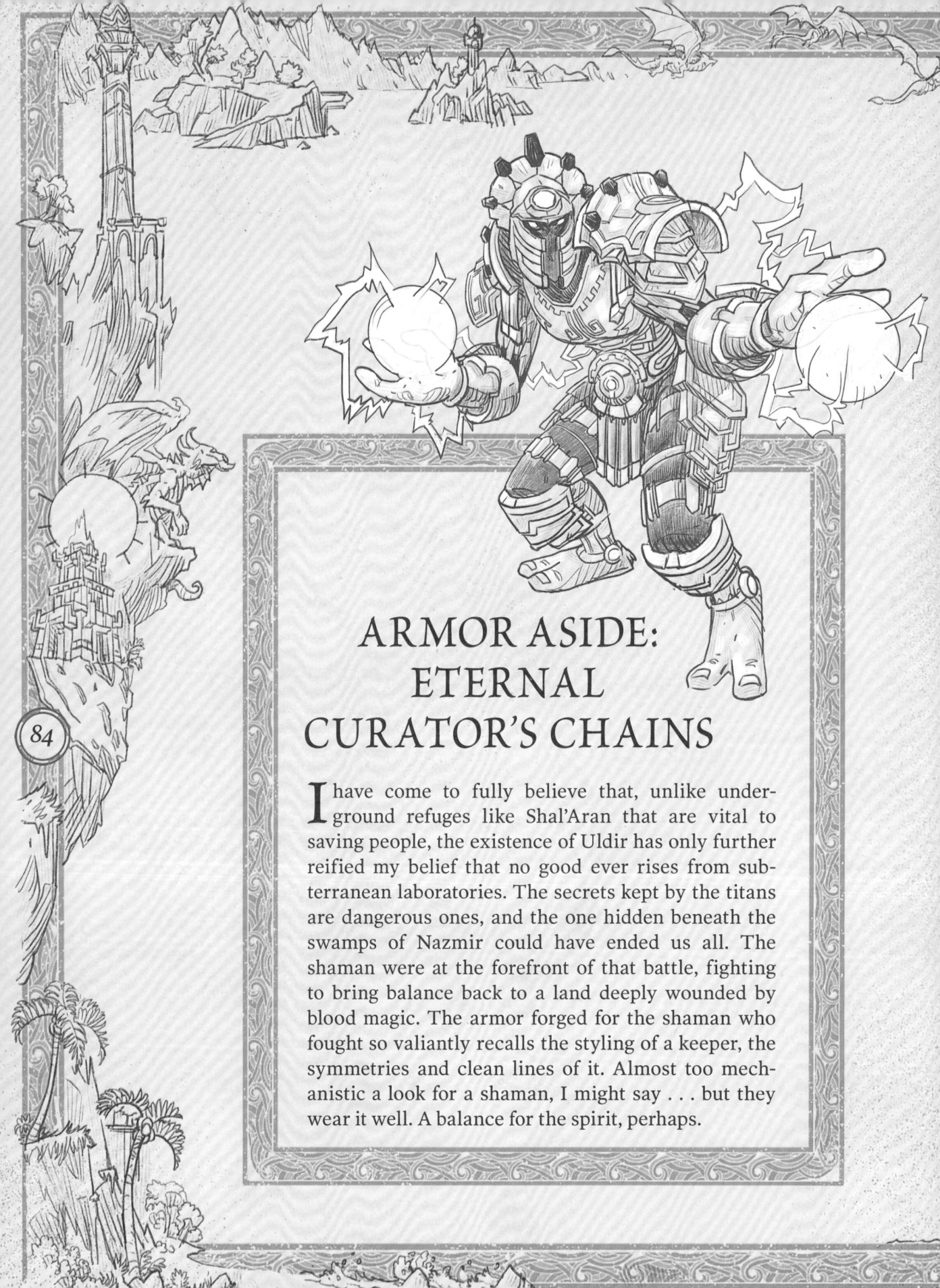

ARMOR ASIDE: ETERNAL CURATOR'S CHAINS

I have come to fully believe that, unlike underground refuges like Shal'Aran that are vital to saving people, the existence of Uldir has only further reified my belief that no good ever rises from subterranean laboratories. The secrets kept by the titans are dangerous ones, and the one hidden beneath the swamps of Nazmir could have ended us all. The shaman were at the forefront of that battle, fighting to bring balance back to a land deeply wounded by blood magic. The armor forged for the shaman who fought so valiantly recalls the styling of a keeper, the symmetries and clean lines of it. Almost too mechanistic a look for a shaman, I might say . . . but they wear it well. A balance for the spirit, perhaps.

COURT OF SPIRITS

I traveled near the coast first, still disquieted and looking for solid evidence of what I had felt. Torga's Rest was also befouled by blood magic long ago. The remains of the tortollans' loa, Torga, have been respectfully interred, but it is still a place of pilgrimage for the tortollans. They haven't made anything so formal as a school or academy there, but it has the air of one, brightly colored tents or simple shacks where young tortollans can meet their elders and sit for story after story, often beside the tiny, reincarnated Torga himself.

Trolls come here now as well to listen and share stories, if in small numbers; Talanji made certain that the tortollan leader Lashk had a seat on the Zanchuli Council, another sign of her determination to right the wrongs of her ancestors. Her people are at least beginning to realize that they have much wisdom and knowledge to contribute—they're as long-lived as we nightborne. I suspect when next I come here, there will be more trolls of more tribes . . . and I hope more people from across the whole of Zandalar.

The ruined ancient palace of Nazwatha, once one of the three seals upon G'huun, brought back that unsettling feeling of shadows and whispers. It seems to be slowly sinking into the swamp, forgotten and unremarked. Looking over its rotting stones, I couldn't help but wish it would sink faster and be buried; the air around it is . . . too still—it feels wrong.

I expected to feel a similar disquiet at the Heart of Darkness (and Uldir within it), which is still surrounded by the rotting remains of the wooden blood troll village. The air of this place is laden with evil deeds, but it is no more wretched than anywhere with such blood-soaked soil might be. Yet it lacks the feeling of stirring and whispers and being *seen* that I felt in the Necropolis and near Nazwatha, even though this is the place where G'huun was created and then slain.

Though the blood trolls were gone, the undead *were not*. I charred a few with spells, but there were too many and I had not been prepared for this kind of fight. I . . . ran. Into the swamp.

It was not the best idea I've had.

Far wiser than pigheadedly standing your ground and fighting them all alone like someone else you might know . . .

FROGMARSH

After what felt like an eternity of slogging through mud and water, tripping over roots, getting bitten by insects, I've decided we are *not* coming anywhere near this place for a vacation, Lor'themar. Even you would be hard-pressed to find something nice to say about it. Fortunately, I felt the call of magic that wasn't familiar, precisely, but similar enough to what I might feel while visiting Val'sharah. I followed this to the Frogmarsh, filled with chirruping frogs that sounded like music.

Look for my next work of poetry, titled "Ode to a Stinking Swamp and the Midges That Drank Half My Blood."

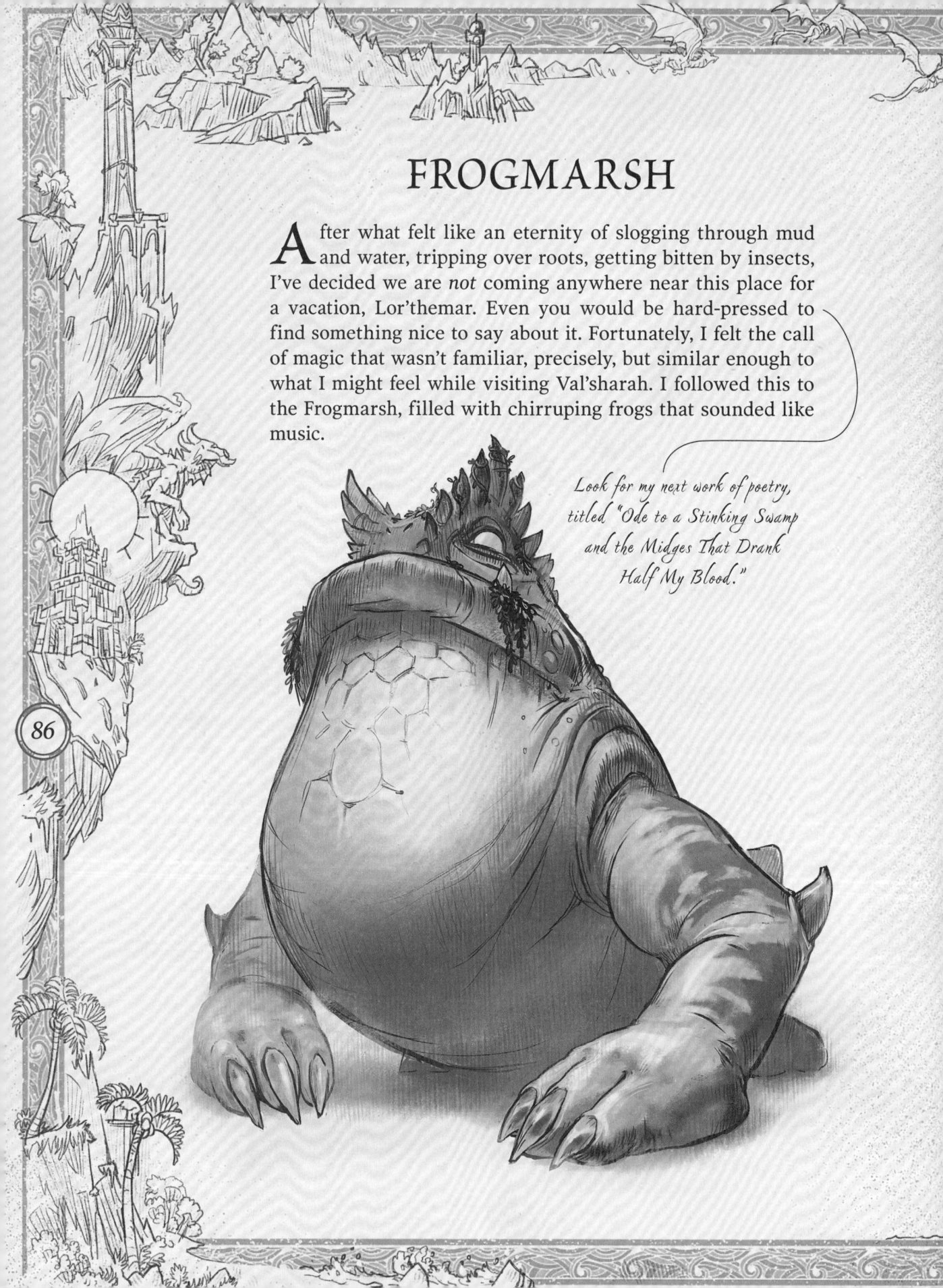

The frog loa Krag'wa had a good laugh at my disheveled state and unhidden misery, but then he had his children rid me of the cloud of bugs that had been trying to make a feast of me. I eagerly accepted when he offered me clean water to wash off the worst of the muck. I thanked him, as one should always be polite to gods if possible. A rainstorm began outside, and as is my wont, I turned the topic to magic. I amused Krag'wa with a few of my tricks enough that he showed me magic of his own, again that familiar-yet-not magic of a wild god.

Best of all, he had one of his larger frog-children take me to the Zul'jan Ruins, with an air of amusement I wouldn't tolerate from anyone but a god. I was just happy, at that point, to be one step closer to dry clothes.

NAZJATAR

I did not intend to go to Nazjatar when I chose Zandalar as my destination. It is perhaps the last place in all of Azeroth I might want to visit, still filled with ghosts and painful memories, reminders of old failings and betrayals that make me feel all too helpless. When I was there before, everywhere I looked were the shades of people I had once known, the ruins of beautiful Zin-Azshari twisted but still recognizable. But with the murmurings I'd heard, the intimation that something might be afoot from Khadgar . . . I feared if there is darkness threatening to swallow us once more, Nazjatar could well be its source, and I could not be at peace with myself without knowing for certain.

I still knew the way, though without the Tidestone, the city was once more beneath the waves. I spent the better part of a morning weaving the spell that could take me into those dark depths, giving me light and air and preventing the water's weight from crushing me; it was a feat that left my head aching.

If I can observe it dispassionately, Nazjatar is a strange amalgamation of memories overprinted on each other. First, the Highborne city I once knew and loved; overprinted by dark magic and water, barnacles and reefs, and so many years; overprinted by its time abruptly in the air again, dotted with the wreckage of Horde and Alliance ships, though the bones of the sailors and soldiers claimed on the reefs have been long since carried away or scattered by tides. Try as I might to hold on to that intellectual observation, all I see are ghosts upon ghosts upon ghosts—but though I looked for Sivara, as if this time I could save my old student or at least fully offer my contrition, I did not see her in the shivering waters. She is one ghost who will remain at my side when I leave Nazjatar.

There was magic in Nazjatar still, giving the depths an eerie and unhealthy glow. Naga remain, now fighting each other as they splinter into ever more factions in the absence of their queen. I still felt Azshara, but her presence is fading, like the heat left behind after a fire has been put out. She is no longer there, which is one relief at least. And the shadows I looked for? The whispers? If there is aught of darkness creeping back into our world, it is not coming through Nazjatar.

Puzzled and glad of it, I departed back to the surface, leaving the drowned ghosts behind. I am sure I will tell Lor'themar of this excursion eventually, as it will no doubt disturb my sleep some night. By then, I can hope that he won't tease me too terribly for being a hypocrite.

There is no power in the world that will keep me from teasing you, love. But in this . . . I won't. I have too many of my own concerns growing, even if I know that I, too, ought to not be thinking about such things.

Truly, I wish you had been there at my side, no matter how much chiding that might have earned. It was . . . difficult to bear.

My love,

Zandalar has been fascinating to visit—and I've seen a great deal more of it now that we're not in the middle of a war. We ought to go places when there isn't a battle set to happen more often. I did not find any one place that met all my criteria for a perfect honeymoon, though I think you would greatly enjoy the Warbeast Kraal and the Garden of the Loa, knowing that you like wilder places. (I've included my notes about several other options so you can read my thoughts in more detail there.) Really, all Zuldazar would be to your liking, so if there is a place you find particularly interesting, I could be . . . convinced to stay and dine among our friends for a time.

All of this is unnecessary detail to dress the truth: I miss you. I found myself wishing for you often as I traveled alone across Zandalar. (Talanji tried to saddle me with a guide quite early on, and I gave her the slip, since we both know I like to do things at my own pace.) I missed you by my side to pause at the sunset or laugh at something silly or hold me close.

Nothing bad has happened—don't wrinkle your brow. But as we both know, where there is light, there is darkness. And there are quite a few places that are not in the least suitable for a vacation.

Your Thalyssra

She will, now that she's had time to unknot herself. Perhaps I've spent too much time thinking of everyone but myself, and released from the bonds of responsibility I've rebounded too far in the other direction. I'm sorry, love.

The only assurance I need is to know you're all right.

KUL TIRAS

It certainly felt strange to be sailing toward an Alliance stronghold without an army at my back and no purpose other than cataloging vacation spots. I'd only read reports about Kul Tiras during the Fourth War—no doubt because there were certain parts of Sylvanas's design that I would have found deeply repugnant—but that's a boon for this visit. I don't carry the baggage of having personally sacked any of the towns, only my traveling pack.

The one thing I find myself disquieted by, looking toward these new shores, is to be sailing away from my wife after only just arriving at her side. While she promised to find me straightaway should I send word to her, this distance between us isn't an emergency . . . only deeply worrying. I'm still not certain what to make of her temper, though I think perhaps the responsibilities of rule have started to weigh on her. (Will she admit as much? She's teased me about my anxieties before, but it's easier to see such things in others than in oneself.) I wish I could have slowed her down from her frenetic pace, but such course would obviously have been the wrong approach. Much as I dislike it, an opportunity to reconsider strategy might help.

-VI-
TIRAGARDE SOUND

While Drustvar is on the side of Kul Tiras that faces the Broken Isles, my ship followed the coast south and around to arrive in Tiragarde Sound. It's the largest region of Kul Tiras, if cut to pieces by a harbor, a massive bay, and quite a few rivers. The harbor is home to the capital Boralus, which is also the nation's largest port. There was no other possible entry point; I'd sent word ahead to the Lord Admiral, to make it clear I wasn't trying to sneak in for some nefarious purpose.

I questioned my decision immediately, with rather wary looks and pointed questions directed at me from the dock. I was left to cool my heels in the customs house for an amount of time that would have driven Thalyssra to distraction, though I took it as an opportunity to do a bit of people- and ship-watching.

Eventually, a young human woman in Proudmoore livery arrived, introduced herself as Lana Varing, and stated very firmly that she would be my guide throughout my travels in Kul Tiras, courtesy of the Lord Admiral herself.

I can take a hint, as much as I might internally rebel at being assigned a minder. "Excellent," I told her. "I hope those boots of yours are well broken in." The quickly masked look of horror on her face was one I am not too good to treasure.

Anyone who thinks you're too straightforward for diplomacy has never seen you gently twist someone into knots for the amusement of it.

BORALUS HARBOR & SOUTHERN TIRAGARDE SOUND

Boralus Harbor is what gives the city its name, one of the best natural harbors I've ever seen—which also offers one of many reasons why the Kul Tirans are so famed for their shipbuilding. With my new minder in tow, I availed myself of the nearest pub and bought several rounds, then gracefully lost an arm-wrestling competition. This seemed to sweeten the general demeanor toward me there, at least, and earned me invitations to see a few ships and shops.

Ultimately, a place not without its charms, but I wouldn't want an extended stay here if I'm supposed to be on vacation, as my wife insists. I'd be spending all my time feeling I had to be diplomatic, a good representative of the blood elves and the Horde. Something more private would be better suited to our needs.

ASHVANE TRADING COMPANY YARDS & DOCKS

The Ashvane Trading Company was once the largest employer in Boralus, though—per all the gossip I acquired thanks to the reasonable price of ale—it was a deeply troubled operation. I'd of course known that the company's former leader, Lady Ashvane, threw in her lot with pirates, plotted a political coup, later turned out to be working for Azshara, and then fully abandoned her position. I was with the Horde when we encountered and slew the strange creature Azshara transformed her into. (If Ashvane had bothered to ask elves of any kind, we could have told her that is the way Azshara rewards all her lackeys in the end.)

In the intervening time, the Proudmoores took over much of what once belonged to the Ashvanes . . . but the manufactory was ceded back to the locals and is now a worker-owned collective. What the company is called now is . . . a mystery I don't care to unravel, as I received multiple answers when I asked. It'll supposedly be put to a vote soon so that people will stop bickering about it.

Whatever they're called, they've drawn much business from the manufacture of arms and munitions, at least since the Second War. I'll admit, it was heartening to hear complaints about sales in that area flagging now that we and the Alliance aren't at each other's throats. They've been forced to branch out into cookware and fireworks for peacetime industries.

Might be worth giving their fireworks a try the next time we've a celebration to conduct in Silvermoon.

PROUDMOORE ACADEMY

I knew I ought to present myself at Proudmoore Keep and get that over with. While yes, my love, I know I'm on vacation, Horde relations with the Alliance in general and Kul Tiras in particular are still fraught. I didn't want anyone reading it as a snub or something nefarious should I avoid the Proudmoores entirely.

Proudmoore Keep is an impressive structure—and I'm rather enamored of the hedge maze. To my relief, I was informed that the Lord Admiral was not currently at home, off doing something that was none of my business to know. I was surprised to then be invited in to have an awkward but not entirely unfriendly tea with the former Lord Admiral, Katherine Proudmoore, who is every bit as icy and impressive as rumor would have it. I conveyed my polite greetings and innocuous pleasantries. Lady Katherine, unprompted, assured me that truly Jaina did regret that she hadn't made it to our wedding, but that her duties had been running her ragged. And in this regard, I do believe her.

That was rather . . . sweet of her.

I was a bit bemused by her then volunteering to give me a brief tour of the Proudmoore Academy, where she's been spending most of her time in non-retirement. The possible purpose of such a tour became clear when I remarked on the numbers of recruits being run through their paces; she mentioned that the navy was well on being rebuilt after the losses in the Fourth War, though she was of course uninterested in offering further, useful detail. It was a show put on for my benefit, and one I certainly hadn't asked for. The stiffness of our conversation melted away as soon as I got her on the subject of sailing, which made the rest of the brief tour much more interesting.

Never doubt how charming you are without even trying, Lor'themar.

MARINER'S ROW

Bolstered by the unexpected welcome at Proudmoore Keep, and at Lady Katherine's recommendation, I took a walk east across the town. Unity Square, just outside the keep, is still overseen by a statue of Daelin Proudmoore. A few plaques indicated that the square was a celebration of the four houses of Kul Tiras . . . but I noted that the banners of House Ashvane are unsurprisingly absent. Someone must have forgotten to update their historical markers.

The more residential parts of the city were a pleasant enough walk: Upton Borough, Crosswind Commons, and then into Mariner's Row after I took a break for a drink and to listen to an excellent bard at the Shark. It was plain that the farther one got from the keep, the lower in the social strata the residents of the houses were, though I wouldn't accuse even the farthest reaches of Mariner's Row of being close to squalid—and it has the newest buildings as well, courtesy of being partially destroyed by us during the Fourth War. I did not feel the need to point this out to anyone.

ARMOR ASIDE: RAZORFIN REGALIA

Armor and weapons are what I'd call a useful way to commemorate a battle for those who were there. Rogues did their part in infiltrating Azshara's palace and stabbing no small number of naga repeatedly in the back while scouting out the path for us to enter the fray. The Razorfin Regalia draws inspiration from the naga felled in these battles. Rather more . . . effervescent than I'd expect a rogue to like to wear, but I suppose the true experts could hide themselves effectively even if they were blazing with light and covered in bells.

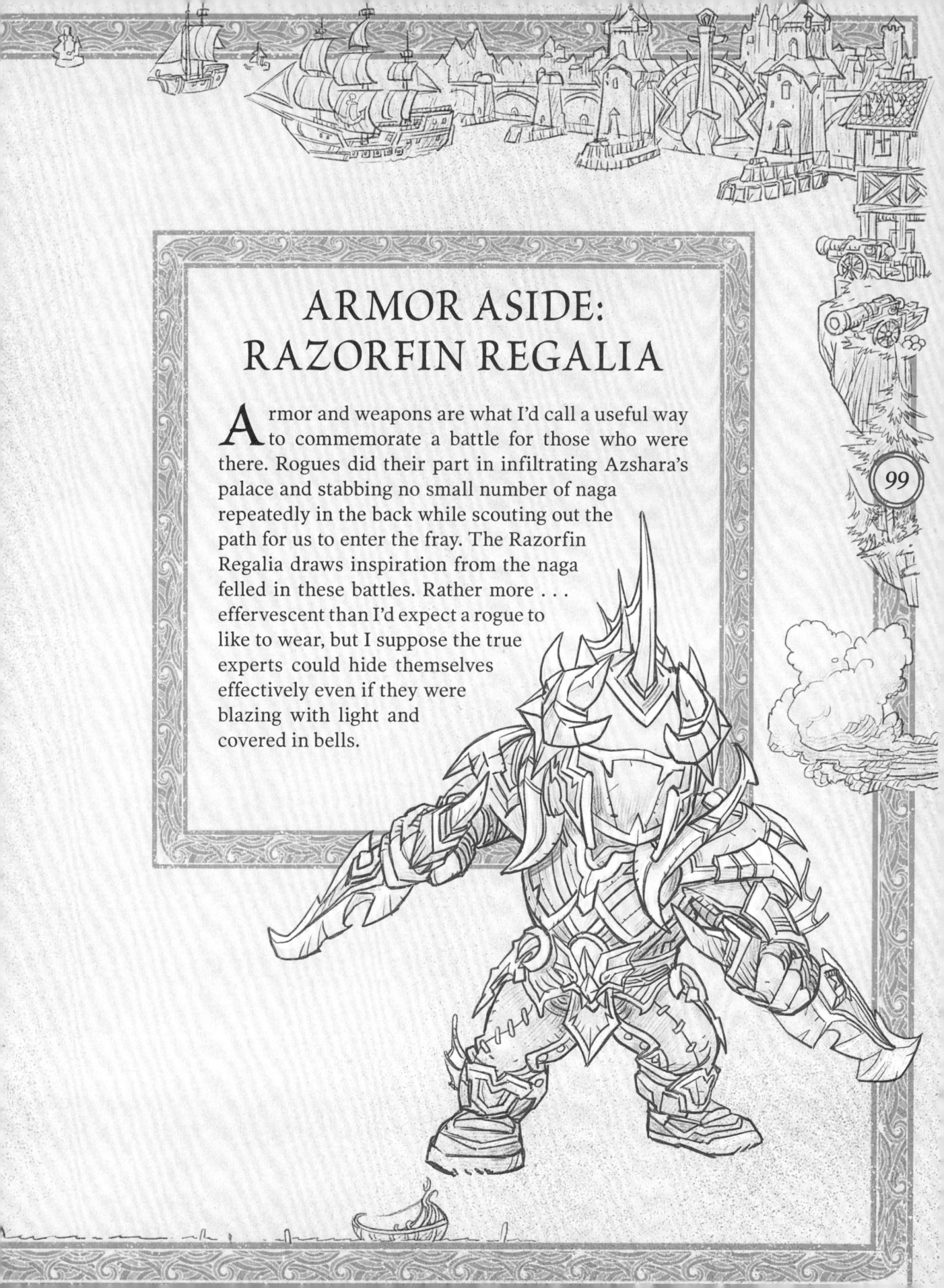

STORMSONG MONASTERY

I took a rowboat over to Stormsong Monastery; they don't allow entrance except by water. It's a rather foreboding place and sparsely populated. I was told by my glowering guide that many Tidesages had given themselves over to the Old Gods, and in the wake of the war there was something of a purge imposed by the Kul Tirans themselves.

Importantly, while I certainly wouldn't call it a fun place to visit, I found no sign of the dark magics the Tidesages had once used, which my chaperone, Miss Varing, did seem to find a relief.

FIZZSPRINGS RESORT

A handbill posted at the Shark convinced me to stop by Fizzsprings Resort once I'd finished my tour of Boralus. It was a relief to get out of the city; even though I stuck out as a blood elf and member of the Horde in Kul Tiras, I immediately felt less scrutinized once I was out on the paths, riding a hired horse. (I'd been offered a mount from the Proudmoore stables but decided that I didn't wish to encroach further on a hospitality that already felt quite tenuous.) I could almost forget Miss Varing trailing me like a disapproving storm cloud.

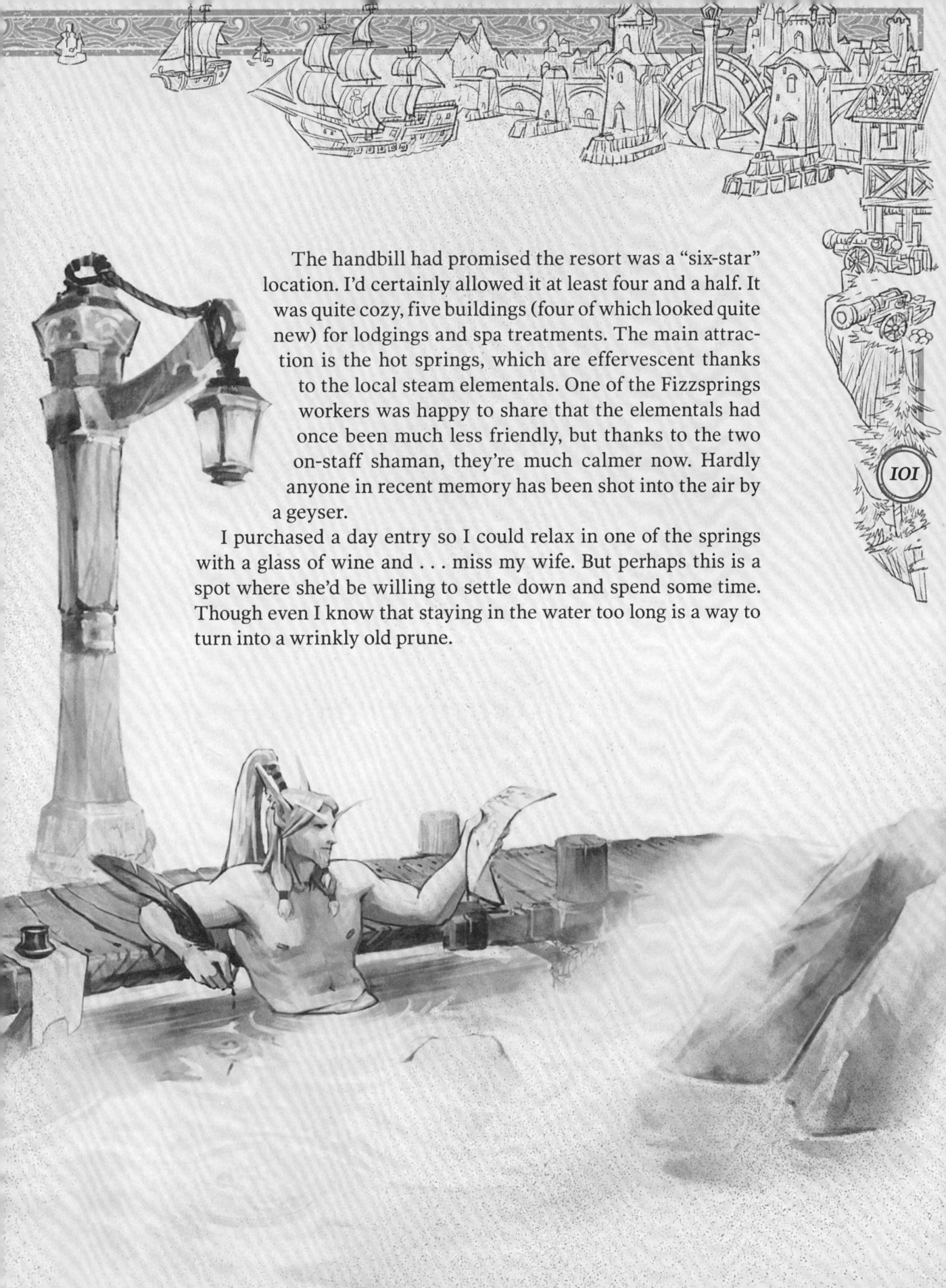

The handbill had promised the resort was a "six-star" location. I'd certainly allowed it at least four and a half. It was quite cozy, five buildings (four of which looked quite new) for lodgings and spa treatments. The main attraction is the hot springs, which are effervescent thanks to the local steam elementals. One of the Fizzsprings workers was happy to share that the elementals had once been much less friendly, but thanks to the two on-staff shaman, they're much calmer now. Hardly anyone in recent memory has been shot into the air by a geyser.

I purchased a day entry so I could relax in one of the springs with a glass of wine and . . . miss my wife. But perhaps this is a spot where she'd be willing to settle down and spend some time. Though even I know that staying in the water too long is a way to turn into a wrinkly old prune.

ANGLEPOINT WHARF

After the fresh and bracing air at the resort, the atmosphere of Anglepoint Wharf was a bit like getting slapped in the face. Between the swirling flocks of gulls and the general stench at the docks, I've little doubt that it is a town built around the trade and packing of fish. There wasn't a horse to be hired in the town, something I should have expected with the nearby festival going on. I managed to hire two surprisingly charming mules for myself and my guide, and we got out of Anglepoint as quickly as possible.

NORWINGTON ESTATE

I'd originally intended to go to Drustvar first, but on a bit of unexpected advice from Lady Katherine, I made way for the Norwington Estate and arrived in time for the penultimate day of the Norwington Equestrian and Hunt Festival, when the highest-level races and dressage competitions were being held. A day of pure joy, watching the Kul Tiran nobility and the much-storied Roughnecks of the Alliance riding some beautiful horses. Not even the Fourth War interrupted the holding of the festival—though I was told that the fifteenth year was very dicey due to the Alliance using the estate grounds to test Azerite weaponry and the Horde causing a bit of destruction when we showed up to steal it.

The Mildenhall Meadery from Stormsong Valley had a booth there that I went to *several* times. I even talked myself into an invitation to tour their grounds, once I made it to the north side of the island. This day was also the culmination of a folk arts competition that included whittled wooden figurines. Of course, I bought one of the little horse carvings for Thalyssra.

If I keep it on my desk, I will think of you every time I look up from a paper or reach for a pen.

ROCKSKIP FALLS & WANING GLACIER

While I'd ended up with mules purely by accident, they turned out to be a serendipitous choice. After being told how lovely the glacial Rockskip Falls are, I decided to see so for myself, since I had a day on my hands before the next ship for Drustvar was to depart.

Glaciers are not terribly common outside of Northrend, and this one had the benefit both of beauty and of not having to worry about unfriendly undead popping out of a crevasse. The path was well maintained, considering it is a road across a floe of moving ice, and it got us to an excellent viewpoint where I could enjoy the falls, with rainbows scintillating in their mists. From here I could also take in the panorama of most of Tiragarde and a bit of Drustvar's east coast. I could see as far to the south as Daelin's Gate, which my guide told me had been rebuilt after being razed by the Irontide Raiders under the traitorous direction of Lady Ashvane.

I sat and simply enjoyed the moment until my guide made an impatient noise so like my dear wife that it made my heart ache a little... and I realized that I had become quite cold.

Lor'themar...

−VII−
DRUSTVAR

A small Kul Tiran cutter on its way to deliver a shipment of fabric took me and my chaperone to the west coast region of Drustvar (thankfully no longer under the thumb of the Irontide Raiders, so we reached our destination without getting our throats slit). Compared to Tiragarde, it's a very inhospitable place, all rugged mountains shrouded in glaciers and thick forests barely cloaking the steep foothills. It looks like a grim illustration from a children's book of tales about phantoms and witches. Fitting, I suppose, given that the land was once terrorized by a quite real coven of witches steeped in death magic.

CORLAIN

Corlain is the capital of Drustvar, though it's out of truth rather than unkindness that I say it barely qualifies as a city. It's more a sprawling series of farmsteads and houses dotted in the forest, with a small walled settlement at the feet of Waycrest Manor. At first glance, it's a rather dark and forbidding place in a way that reminds me of the Dead Scar... Do enough death magic in an area and it leaves an imprint on the very atmosphere, though I'm certain Thalyssra would offer a more technical explanation than that. After talking to a few locals in the tavern, I came to understand that this place is downright cheery compared to how Corlain was before the fall of the Heartsbane Coven.

Waycrest Manor, the home of House Waycrest, is open as a house once more, under the guidance of Lucille Waycrest, though much of the grounds and interior have, according to the locals, been gutted by the Order of Embers to clean out the taint of the witches.

This strange, Drust-sourced magic the coven had and the curses they laid seemed to me like something Thalyssra would be very interested in, but the new Lady Waycrest has prioritized destroying all remnants and records of the witches' work rather than remodeling her home... Understandable, considering the involvement of her mother in the whole affair.

I contented myself with a tour of the aviary instead, the pride and joy of Corlain. They had quite a few fine falcons there. I wish I'd had time to hunt.

WHITEGROVE CHAPEL

Whitegrove Chapel is a lovely little building on the western cliffs not far from Waycrest Manor, with a view of the Western Watch lighthouse. At night, the curtain of its lights dances across the horizon. Another place we could renew our vows, I think. I'm a romantic enough fool that I had a bit of a daydream about kissing my wife while watching those dancing lights.

After we have our honeymoon first, of course!

Since this writing, I have been informed that the last two weddings at the chapel ended in assassination and murder. So... perhaps not.

I'd normally laugh about superstition, but in this case, I'd rather be safe than sorry.

FALLHAVEN

As sprawling as Corlain is, I thought I might have trouble finding Arom's Stand. But following the road, it has a bit of a wall and straddles Highroad Pass through the mountains, so it's quite hard to miss. On the other side of the mountains lies its sister village of Fallhaven. Out of a dark curiosity I visited both; they'd been extensively cursed by the now-gone witches, and I wanted to see what mark might have been left behind. I promise that I was relieved to discover that the people have all been restored to their un-cursed selves, though I was treated to some frankly hair-raising accounts of what it had been like after buying a few rounds at the tavern. Some of the cursed had been stuck in time, still as statues, while others were unable to speak and only performed the same actions over and over again. The place has recovered well now, bustling with tradesfolk and a newly opened ceramics kiln, but I also noticed a certain wariness among many of the folk who must have lived through the bad time. I know well that not all scars are visible to the eye.

ARMOR ASIDE: LURKING DEFILER'S SCALEMAIL

The events in Zandalar and Kul Tiras were ultimately what led to the release of N'Zoth, despite our best efforts. It was for the champions of both Horde and Alliance to stand against N'Zoth and its minions, and for that they took the battle to Ny'alotha, the Waking City. Hunters often serve as the vanguard in battle, scouting ahead, no matter the environment. The Lurking Defiler's Scalemail celebrates their part of the victory against Ny'alotha; the glowing eye on the belt is rather a macabre trophy—and one I might wonder at the wisdom of, considering how the Old Gods seem to . . . echo.

CRIMSON FOREST

I was repeatedly assured that the Crimson Forest is now a safe place before venturing in... to the extent that I began to wonder if I looked like a hapless old man or someone with a nervous disposition to the people in Arom's Stand. (Miss Varing, I will note, was less than pleased that I insisted on exploring the forest but could think of no good reason to stop me.) I think the frequent affirmations are more their own memories of terror speaking to reassure themselves that the coven is truly gone.

The local farmers still do not often venture inside, even though it is a perfectly lovely forest to my eye, dominated by the red-foliaged trees and equally red ground-covering plants for which it is named. I did find the Drust ruins I'd been told of, largely destroyed now. The hollow tree that once served as an entrance to the Blighted Lands has been burned to ash and a few spikes of charred wood. I found no sign that the doorway persisted, something I was certain to pass on at my next stop, Falconhurst, since I feel the people of Drustvar need as much reassurance as they can get.

FLETCHER'S HOLLOW

I would have done the same.

I intended to go straight to Fletcher's Hollow as another possible vacation spot, but a traveler on the road through the mountains mentioned the Drust ruins of Gol Koval buried in the glacier. I am sorry, Thalyssra, but I couldn't pass those by without a look in to make certain all was well. There isn't much left to those ruins, merely a few carved stones in the clutches of the glacier, though I did find a partial scroll that looked to be a remnant of the witches. I took that as a gift for my favorite scholar of all things magic.

Fletcher's Hollow is another quaint village, though it is far more compact than Fallhaven or Corlain, because it is built around a mine. I stopped for a warm drink in the Rusty Bucket Tavern (the glasses were much cleaner than the name implies) and inquired after a boat rental to get myself and Miss Varing back to Anglepoint Wharf (and from there on to Stormsong Valley).

Aethas will be mortified to know that he has slipped so far in your affections.

Then he ought to have taken up poetry and kissing if he wanted not to be supplanted.

AUTUMNVALE

It was too late in the day to rent a boat to reach Anglepoint Wharf, so I found rooms for the night and passed the rest of the afternoon looking through the hunting grounds to the north in Autumnvale.

Glenbrook Hunting Grounds made me wish I'd brought my bow with me for the sheer enjoyment of a hunt—I could have even handed the fresh meat over to the proprietor of the Rusty Bucket in thanks, if nothing else—though I imagine my guide would have found it alarming. She certainly found it more than alarming when we were attacked by what looked like a deer at first glance, though it became obvious that it had a skull in place of a head and fire for eyes. We'd been warned that hexed animals still wandered the forests, and one had finally found us.

I snatched my sword off my minder's belt and beheaded the creature, though not before it gave me a nasty nick on my left arm. I did pointedly apologize when I offered the sword back to her, since there hadn't been time to ask to use it politely . . . and the deer had seemed quite interested in goring her.

She told me to keep the sword. Point finally made.

–VIII–
STORMSONG VALLEY

With my tour of Drustvar completed (generally: not a honeymooning spot, otherwise a fascinating place to visit), Stormsong Valley was next on my list. Neither Miss Varing nor I were particularly thrilled to have our noses assaulted by Anglepoint Wharf for the third time in less than a fortnight, but our foray was at least short. There was a fishing boat headed toward Thresher's Wharf on the west side of the valley, and that was good enough for my purposes.

Stormsong Valley stands in sharp contrast to the other provinces of Kul Tiras precisely because of its softness, its rolling green hills visible even from the slightly slimy deck of an approaching trawler. It is home to countless farmsteads, its climate purportedly perfect for growing the bulk of Kul Tiras's food. Yet somehow this makes the mountains that protect it—and the rocky spit that's home to the Shrine of the Storm to the east—seem even more foreboding.

The nearest settlement to Thresher's Wharf is Millstone Hamlet, a charming little place that thankfully had a total of four horses available to hire out and was willing to let me have half their stock. Before we could depart for more populated areas, however, I caught the delicious scent of baking bread wafting on the breeze and followed my nose unerringly to its source: a bakery. It was a quaint place, run by a family (wife and children, with the husband being the one who milled the flour, I was informed), who were more than happy to sell me a fresh loaf and a bit of cheese to go with it. I split the bread with Miss Varing as we rode away; it didn't even want for butter. Now *that* is something I wish I could bring to Thalyssra, but bread is never as good the second day.

We shall have to find time to go there together.
A stolen moment for a picnic, perhaps?

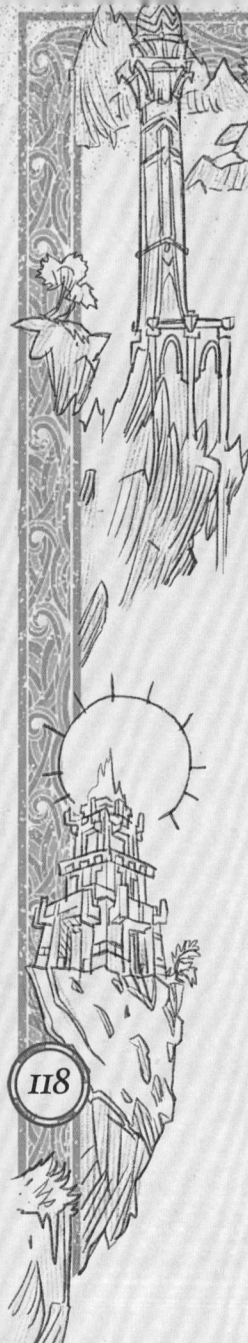

BRENNADAM

The approach to Brennadam put me in mind of Corlain. Like Corlain, Brennadam is the regional capital, but it is spread into sprawling farmsteads so that the core of the town proper seems much smaller and less populated than it truly is.

I certainly received a much colder welcome in Brennadam than I had in Corlain. As my guide tersely reminded me, the Horde had nearly destroyed the town during the Fourth War, so I could see the motivations of such ire. Likely, the way the people of Drustvar still have nightmares about their witches and fear their return, it's the Horde that haunts the dreams of the people in Stormsong Valley.

While this reminder made it easier to empathize with the way the citizens felt and to put on my good diplomat face, it did *not* help me when it came to finding accommodations for the night. (Striking this one too from the list of possible honeymoon spots, to be sure.)

MILDENHALL MEADERY

I had determined I would go to Mildenhall Meadery after seeing them at the Norwington Estate, and I was not disappointed! The meadery rests in a part of the valley that smells sweet with honey; it's floral without being quite strong enough to go from pleasant to cloying. I can't imagine how many hives they must have.

We joined a tour of the meadery operations, got to taste a bit of honeycomb and the meadery's famous ravenberry tarts, and then were turned loose in the mead hall to sample as many meads as we had coin and will to try. I ordered several cases of mead to be shipped back to the Broken Isles.

The conversation in the mead hall was not quite so light and sweet, however. A rather drunken man warned me and my guide about a darkness on the move across Stormsong, ancient enemies stirring. Miss Varing dismissed him as a sot; I didn't find him so easy to put from my mind. I'd already heard of the troubles Kul Tiras has had with the Old Gods; there are even temples of theirs located here, though supposedly not in active use. I will keep an ear to the ground, but as I swore to you no work, I won't go looking.

These, too, ought to come on the picnic we must someday have.

MARINER'S STRAND

Mariner's Strand was a real treat for me; it's home to the Addington Shipyards, which are said to be some of the largest dry docks in Kul Tiras—and here, there were two ships under construction, both designs I was not familiar with. Miss Varing admitted that Kul Tiras has expanded the shipyards; they're rebuilding their navy after losing so many ships, though she remained very tight-lipped about further details.

Through a stroke of sheer luck, my visit coincided with that of Lord Admiral Jaina Proudmoore herself. I wasn't certain exactly what sort of luck it was as she approached and Miss Varing saluted. To call my relationship with the Lord Admiral contentious is a laughable understatement, though I have tried my hardest over the last eight years to build bridges, however tenuous. While Jaina didn't look entirely pleased to see me, she was more wary than anything else—and notably weary as well. To my surprise, she invited me to sit with her awhile and observe the construction of the ships, and she even shared a few points about Kul Tiran ship-building with me as she relaxed into our conversation.

I was admittedly a bit saddened when she was called away to attend the business of the Lord Admiral . . . and remarkably, I think she might have been as well.

Truly, my love, you must have been pining unto death for company to be so charmed by Jaina Proudmoore.

SAGEHOLD

From the abandoned encampment of Warfang, I couldn't help but drag Miss Varing up Stormwatch Peak, where the goats, bandicoons, and rabbits regarded us curiously but otherwise let us be. Stormwatch offers a commanding view of the valley below—including Sagehold.

I'll admit to a little trepidation approaching Sagehold, since I'm aware that the Horde attacked it during the war, and I'd already had such a cold welcome at Brennadam. Surprisingly, there was only the background level of wariness, a general rather than specific distrust of the Horde. I wandered the town—which was rather rustic, with all the wood buildings—before settling in at the tavern for a warm meal and to buy a few rounds of drinks in the hopes of getting the gossip to flow.

I quickly realized that the lack of fear of the Horde was largely because they'd been overrun with k'thir and n'raqi for quite some time before that; just a bit of terrorizing from regular enemies wouldn't be a relief, exactly, after struggling with creatures of the Old Gods, but something close to it. I asked gently about the rumors I'd heard at Mildenhall. *That* was a subject no one wanted to talk about; I gathered that since so many Tidesages had been found to be followers of Azshara and purged, the paranoia of Old God corruption still runs rampant.

WARFANG HOLD

Still thinking about the gossip I heard at the meadery—I know, my love, I know—I made my way to Warfang Hold on the vague notion that if there was any Horde presence, perhaps they'd have information. As serious as Baine has been about the drawdown and keeping the process of peace with the Alliance moving, I ought to have known it had been decommissioned.

A bit odd, wandering around an old Horde base, seeing buildings that look like miniatures sent from Orgrimmar, and knowing that for once they were empty by choice and not by violence. An oddness that ought to be welcomed until it's normal, Baine would say, and I'm sure he'd be right. (I've just made myself feel old.)

THE DROWNED LANDS

Deadwash is certainly a colorful name for a town ... and "the Drowned Lands" an incongruous one for the green, rolling farmlands around it. Miss Varing explained that the lands had been purposefully drained via a seawall at Fort Daelin because more farmlands were needed. Interesting as a marvel of engineering, I suppose, but I would have preferred to see whole ships sailing on the waters.

I did, however, cajole Miss Varing into taking a look at two wrecked ships that stuck incongruously up from the green of the young grain fields—a testament to how this whole expanse had been at the bottom of an inlet. The ships were picked quite clean of anything valuable and every bit of easily removable metal. I've no idea now what they might have been called; their nameplates and figureheads were long gone, unsurprisingly. Some enterprising farmer had even begun to cannibalize wood from one of the ships; I didn't see anyone in the act, but it was plain from the way a patch of deck was missing, the scars of its removal fresh.

I took my lunch there, sitting in the shade of the gently rotting ship, and noticed that locals had also taken to carving their initials or names with those of their lovers or (sometimes delightfully rude) messages into the planks.

Of course, I added my and Thalyssra's names. One must respect tradition, after all!

Yes, "tradition." Of which you are a well-known, dutiful follower. But I won't claim to be displeased by you having me there with you, even in a small way.

THE SHRINE OF THE STORM

While supposedly purified, the Shrine of the Storm is still an uncanny place, and I feel no shame at all in saying that. From the moment I landed there on a gryphon, I was unsettled. I felt my breath shorten in my chest on approach, not out of beauty but an elemental dread of the sort that would have had me readying my bow and looking for something large and hungry when I was a ranger.

Yet despite the general brooding and disturbing air of the place—and its known connections to the Old Gods—I caught no hints of whispers or shadows of the sort I've learned to look out for, even at the charmingly named Precipice of Oblivion. It seems to now be the home of genuine and earnest Tidesages.

I left quickly once I'd satisfied myself that I didn't need to go hunting for trouble across the mist-damp stones. My gryphon also seemed quite eager to be shot of the place. We ended the day at Braxton Lodge, a place that had been (if at times begrudgingly) recommended to me multiple times while I'd been at Brennadam.

The lodge looks very new; the proprietor, a lovely woman named Aubrey, told me that it had been all but destroyed by an avalanche and an Azerite wound during the Fourth War, but it had been her family's ambition to get it rebuilt and reopened. It is very cozy now, perfect for a perpetually snowy mountainside, every room with a warm fire and comfortable furniture—and the fare, while relatively plain, is delicious. I could have stayed for a week to simply look at the snows. This, I shall have to mention to Thalyssra . . . though thinking on it, I fear she'd grow quickly bored.

It does sound a delightful place to retreat and find quiet.
I . . . need to allow myself to have quiet first, I suppose.
Perhaps I could, with you.

ARMOR ASIDE: FRILLED HARBINGER'S VESTMENTS

I see shades of Highborne design in the armor made for those who fought against Azshara, and it sits with me strangely to see the elements of the naga in it as well, a reminder of what they came from and at whose hand. It is beautiful when taken by itself, and I see a poetry in taking Azshara's defeat and making it into the vestments of the priests who healed their fellow champions and lashed their enemies with Light and shadow.

MECHAGON

I've heard quite a bit about Mechagon and read a bit more: a titan vault opened by a mad king, his insatiable desire to turn everyone into clockwork imitations of life. Knowing what we do now about the titans and the Curse of Flesh from the Old Gods, King Mechagon's aims make a horrid kind of sense—and I've no small respect for Prince Erazmin successfully leading a resistance against it.

The strangeness of Mechagon starts even with the ship out to the island. Rather than a graceful cutter or a wallowing war galley, it was an entirely mechanical affair, dizzying to look at and inscrutable the way I find most gnomish or goblin technology to be. The gnome engineer on the ship, a young lady named Niffy who looked to be about half mechanical herself, was happy to explain everything to me in detail as soon as she realized I was the least bit curious. Did I understand even a tenth of it? No, but it certainly made the voyage pass quickly, and what I did learn about gnomish wind-generators for sails was *fascinating*. The conversation had just begun to move on to submarines—a topic of extreme enthusiasm for Niffy, who seemed to know all of the statistics on how fast and far they could go—when we arrived.

RUSTBOLT

According to young Niffy, Rustbolt has come quite a way since its time as the home of the Rustbolt Resistance, when it was a glorified garbage dump that the rebels hid in, cobbling together machines and weapons from the drifts of junk. To my eye, it was still quite chaotic, but I could tease out method to the clutter. The town certainly has the air of a cheery seaside trading port; an interesting place to explore, but I daresay Thalyssra would find it more interesting than myself. Arcanists seem to like tinkering quite a bit, even if their medium is more magic and less metal. I bought her a few clever little trinkets that looked like they might be fun to take apart.

In some sense, it is all mathematics in the end.

MECHAGON CITY

Mechagon City feels like a grander version of Rustbolt, dug deep into the soil and rock; it has the same sort of chaos, magnified by the larger population, though I could tell in this case that much of the mess was a matter of cleanup and rebuilding.

Niffy, who'd accompanied Miss Varing and me to the city, enthusiastically detailed the various urban renewal projects that were being run by Prince Erazmin with the approval and aid of King Mekkatorque in Gnomeregan. The Junkwatt Depot has had its more toxic waters cleaned and cleared out, while the large junkyard run by Bondo Bigblock is . . . about as welcoming as a junkyard can be, I suppose.

I'll admit I have a limit to how interesting I can find piles of scrap and bins of bits and bobs, but I was very impressed in the city proper by the Machinist's Garden. Niffy told me in hushed tones that it had once been a literal death trap (and to my eye could still be one if the city required defense), but it was now a very pleasant sort of urban garden, filled with plants and trees that were half mechanical.

The High Tinkertory was my last stop in the city; I was only able to take a peek since I hadn't introduced myself as anything beyond a curious visitor. The former seat of King Mechagon's power is now home to a portal to Stormwind City—which I carefully kept my distance from—and is the place where mechagnome hopefuls embark on their journey to the outside world as adventurers. It was a lovely sight, and Niffy looked rather wistful, watching a young one depart through the portal. I asked her: "Do you miss Stormwind?"

She shook her head. "I had a different path to the outside world . . . I was always a sailor. But I miss my best friend, who's in the Alliance navy now. Our ships don't cross paths very often, and neither of us is much for writing letters. Sometimes I wonder if I popped through, if I'd catch her at port in Stormwind."

"What would you do then?" I asked.

"She'd drag me around the whole city and show me all the fun stuff she's found. It's hard, trying to cram months of adventures into two or three days. Means you don't get a lot of rest. But it's also just not the same doing things when you're alone, you know?"

I wondered if there was a bit of that to Thalyssra's restlessness. If I'd been too . . . stationary for her tastes. "I suppose that's true. Though once you hit a certain age, perhaps you'll have had enough adventures and simply want to have a nice meal and a long talk."

"Mister, you don't appear *that* old." She squinted at me. "So where would you go, if you had a magic portal like that?"

That I very well could have a magic portal if I wanted made the question all the more ironic. "I'd go to wherever my wife is." I smiled at the thought. "And then let her drag me all around and show me the wonderful stuff she's found."

My guiding star,

I have had a wonderful time in Kul Tiras—despite the best efforts of my Proudmoore-provided guide. I hope Zandalar has been equally delightful; I'm entertaining a little dream that as I write this letter to you, you are writing one to me.

While the whole of Kul Tiras was quite fascinating, and I found some spots with strange arcane happenings that would fascinate you, I think there are few standout places that would suit well for an actual honeymoon. I missed you most keenly at the Norwington Estate, where they were having an excellent festival . . . though we'd need to wait a year to do that together, which is a less appealing thought. The whole of Stormsong Valley and its Mildenhall Meadery were also delightful and quiet, as one would like a honeymoon to be. We would just avoid the . . . squiddy bits. I have quite a few more suggestions for when we meet up and compare notes. In fact, where shall we meet? The Broken Isles is perhaps the shortest sailing distance . . .

With all my love,
Lor'themar

My love,

Dream or not, your fancy that we were writing each other at the same time seems close to the truth. I am eager to see you again. As to where we shall meet . . . I fear that the moment I set foot ashore at the Broken Isles, people with "just a small matter" will sense my return and be on me like starving dogs.

Pandaria is the next nearest to Zandalar, but I know you have been there before—and amid a dark time for your people at that. Someplace new to us both would be most welcoming . . . Let us go to the Dragon Isles! I have wanted to see those shores since the flights returned to them. The isles are relatively close to Kul Tiras, and I can ask Pa'ku the Windmother for some aid with the winds to ensure my ship sails swiftly.

I will see you soon, my love. I promise.

Your Thalyssra

⇥ DRAGON ISLES ⇤

I have heard much of the fabled Dragon Isles, but only from the dry reports and missives of our forward expedition. From what I've learned, I don't even know where to begin my imaginings. What sort of place could possibly be equal to the dragons? What will it look like, abandoned for so many thousands of years and only returned to life so recently? These are questions I ask myself . . . when I am not thinking more that each day, each hour, brings me closer to reuniting with Lor'themar—for he is more in my thoughts than the distraction of dragons. Perhaps the Dragon Isles are a place best for that as well—reunions and new beginnings.

This time, let it work. Let me find the source of my disquiet and overcome it.

–IX–
THE WAKING SHORES

The Waking Shores are as raw and beautiful a sight as I could have imagined for the home of the dragons. The volcanoes that heralded the dragons' return are still erupting, steam and smoke shimmering in the air around them, lava running ceaselessly into the sea. I unerringly spotted Lor'themar waiting for me at the docks and was nearly overcome by the emotion of the moment. I know not if my heart has calmed completely in his absence, but seeing him was like touching magic for the first time again, an electricity of the soul that called me unerringly to its source.

More surprisingly, he wasn't waiting alone—Wrathion was with him, looking as puckish as ever despite his new title of diplomat. Wrathion patiently waited for us to embrace, then even apologized once more for the disturbance at our wedding. "Truly, think nothing of it," Lor'themar assured him. "It's given us a good story to tell."

Wrathion explained that he'd come on behalf both of himself and Alexstrasza to show us around the isles. Truly, I could think of no better guide!

ARMOR ASIDE: VIRTUOUS SILVER CATAPHRACT

Champions from both Horde and Alliance aided Alexstrasza and the dragonflights in trying to stop Raszageth from releasing the other Incarnates. They fought their way through Primalist forces in the Vault of the Incarnates at great risk and slew Raszageth in a battle that took every ounce of strength and cunning. Armor commemorating that battle carries a certain callback to the primal energies the champions survived. For paladins, the Virtuous Silver Cataphract shares some of the texture of primal stone, suiting the protective role that paladins of all callings fulfill.

SKYTOP OBSERVATORY

The Skytop Observatory was the first place Wrathion chose to take us, though the only reason he gave was its commanding view of the Waking Shores, from where we might glimpse all that this corner of the isles had to offer. Perhaps more importantly, it is where adventurers of all types learn to ride drakes. Wrathion soon revealed two drakes for our own personal use, as he said it would make our tour of the isles much easier. I don't know if I've seen Lor'themar so delighted since our wedding, and that sight alone was enough to make this entire journey worth it. One smile, one precious moment.

RUBY LIFE POOLS & RUBY LIFESHRINE

The Ruby Lifeshrine is filled with life, yes, but in a different way from those places touched by the Emerald Dream or tended by druids. I've never seen so many precious whelplings, nor could I have imagined so many eggs being eagerly attended to. And this, I know, is a recent development for the dragons, and for that they have my joy as well.

Lor'themar set aside his dignity to be dragged into a game of hide-and-seek with the whelplings. (He lost more than he won, and I am certain that is entirely a result of him throwing the game; he's far too good at hiding.)

I wandered a bit restlessly and spoke to several of the attendants, then ended up on one of the shrine's many overlooks. There, I came across a dragon wearing a dwarven visage, with the gruff voice of an elder. He introduced himself as Veritistrasz when I sat next to him, and we talked awhile. He was one of the dragons who had been born on the isles and left, only to return now to find everything changed and most of his friends long dead. I told him of my Suramar, the similar dislocation I felt—and the even more disturbing glimpse I'd gotten of Nazjatar.

He told me: "When coming home after a long journey, sometimes the place and the people have indeed changed. But standing here, now, I've come to find *I'm* the one who's changed. I'm not the dragon who left these isles thousands of years ago. You're not the Highborne who was driven from Suramar. The battle changes us . . . but so does life. Life is nothing but change."

He was right, a thing I'd thought about myself from time to time. I mentioned my travels with Lor'themar and even admitted to my restlessness, my inability to find a place to settle on, even for a honeymoon.

"Might be because it's not the place that matters so much," he said, squinting out to the horizon. "It's the people you're with that makes it vacation or home or whatnot. And the person you let yourself be when free of expectation."

I made them work for it, dearest, but letting them find me was far more fun than winning the game.

OBSIDIAN CITADEL

The Obsidian Citadel is a sprawling, intimidating affair, though much of that is the natural impression the scent of brimstone and boiling lava leaves. The cheerful greetings called out to Wrathion at our approach lit up the atmosphere immediately. Really, I was bemused to see Wrathion so relaxed among his own people; it was not until I saw him so that I realized what tension he had always carried with him before.

I teased him about it, when there was a quiet moment to watch a few black whelplings play. It was plain to me, then, that he'd brought us here because he wanted to show off what the black dragonflight had become. He offered me a smile far more crooked than his usual one and said: "After standing alone for so long . . . it takes time to learn to be with other people. To give and take. Sometimes, I'm still very bad at it. But it was a lesson worth learning." And then he laughed at *me* and said I looked like I'd been struck by an arrow.

The citadel is now entirely repaired from the damage it took during the djaradin siege, something Wrathion was particularly proud of. He also made certain we had a chance to speak with Ebyssian. It has been only a few years since we last saw each other, but becoming Aspect of the black dragonflight has not changed him—even if it will take getting used to, thinking of him as a dragon rather than his tauren visage.

WINGREST BAY

With proper greetings taken care of for now, Wrathion took us on a rapid flying tour around the Waking Shores, fully indulging Lor'themar's enthusiasm for flight. Wrathion explained that there were a great many aerial courses around the isles that dragons and adventurers alike used for the purposes of racing, with timekeeping overseen by keepers of the bronze dragonflight.

Pardon me, but I believe I also heard you whooping with glee. And Wrathion! He about sounded like a giddy child.

We did not quite race ourselves (though give Lor'themar a few more days to get to know his drake and he soon will), but we saw a few dragons whipping through the air currents. In this rapid style, we flew over Wingrest Bay, the Crumbling Life Archway (a gorgeous place for a picnic at some later point), the Overflowing Rapids, and the verdant green of the Wild Preserve and Apex Canopy.

We did stop at the Uktulut Backwater, a tuskarr village named, I suppose, for its isolation. It is built on a set of lovely waterfalls, and there we indulged in what the tuskarr called "improvised" sushi and anchovy crisps.

Our tour of the Waking Shores ended at Scalecracker Keep, another dragon stronghold that had been besieged by the djaradin before they were defeated by the black dragonflight. Evidence of its siege was still apparent in broken walls and wayward stones; its restoration is no doubt a lesser priority than the Obsidian Citadel itself.

-X-
OHN'AHRAN PLAINS

The Ohn'ahran Plains are like an ocean of grass, gently rolling hills stretching as far as the eye can see. Perfect for grazing animals, herds of plainstompers, mammoths, and more roam anywhere one looks. Roaming centaur can be seen everywhere, moving in caravans or galloping through the grass in smaller hunting parties. The first time Lor'themar caught sight of hawks stooping on the hunt, he let out a whoop. This is a land that suits him perfectly, and watching the weight of his responsibilities fully fall away as he considered the hunts he could go on suited me nicely as well.

Puts me in mind of Stormsong Valley, in a way. Though their lands are more suited to growing wheat and vegetables. There aren't nearly so many herds—nor as much hunting.

MIREWOOD FEN

We passed over Cascades Canyon and its series of waterfalls on our way to the easternmost stretches of the plains. Mirewood Fen stands as an odd place in this landscape, a near-swamp that is dark and overgrown with trees. At the edge of the fen are Timberstep Outpost, a small settlement of friendly centaur, and the tunnel that Fyrakk melted down into Zaralek Cavern, called Iridikron's Gambit since all know at whose behest it was made. Rather than stop at either place, Wrathion led us west to fly over the Clearwater Basin ("Not terribly interesting unless either of you would care to fish.") and to Maruukai, the capital of the Maruuk centaur. As a courtesy, we introduced ourselves there to their Khanam Matra and were officially welcomed. Sarest told us, bemused, that visits such as ours have become very common, something she could not have believed possible only a few years ago—but the centaur have, for the most part, adapted well to the changes of the dragons returning to the isles and bringing the rest of Azeroth with them. At least so long as we mind our manners and respect their domain and traditions.

HORN OF DRUSAHL

I am not an expert on war horns, but the Horn of Drusahl is certainly the largest I have ever seen. I'm uncertain if it is made from wood or from the spiraling horn of some unimaginably large creature; knowing it is a symbol of the pact between the centaur and the green dragonflight, perhaps the answer is both. The Primalist Koroleth captured the centaur's god-spirit Ohn'ahra and forced her to allow the Nokhud leader to blow the horn, thus luring the green dragons into a trap and resulting in the death of Solethus—an act Wrathion was visibly angry about when he related it to us. While Solethus has his own grave marker within the Emerald Gardens, the centaur have placed a memorial for him at the horn as well, to mark their shame at the betrayal of the Nokhud and their own grief at the dragon's death.

Almost an afterthought of the Nokhud's betrayal, the Shikaar Highlands lie just southeast and across the river from the Horn of Drusahl; the Shikaar Clan home was all but obliterated when it was taken over by the Nokhud but has now been rebuilt.

TEERAKAI & THE ETERNAL KURGANS

Part of the lands of Teerakai, the seat of Clan Teerai, looks oddly bumpy from the air. These are burial mounds, which the centaur call the Eternal Kurgans. For what amounts to a massive graveyard, it is a soft and verdant place, which seems fitting for a people so closely allied with the green dragonflight. Wrathion observed that the Eternal Kurgans had been troubled a few years previously by necromancers of Clan Ukhel attempting to resurrect and capture the ancestor spirits to assist their Clan Nokhud allies. The spirits have since been laid back to rest, though faint wisps of memory and whispers of song on the breeze remain; this, it seems, is how it should be.

Nearby Windsong Rise, to the east, is another site of conflict against the Primalists. This is where they captured Ohn'ahra, to be taken to the Horn of Drusahl. The windswept hilltop still shows a spiraling pattern settled into its grasses and ornaments laced about the rocks.

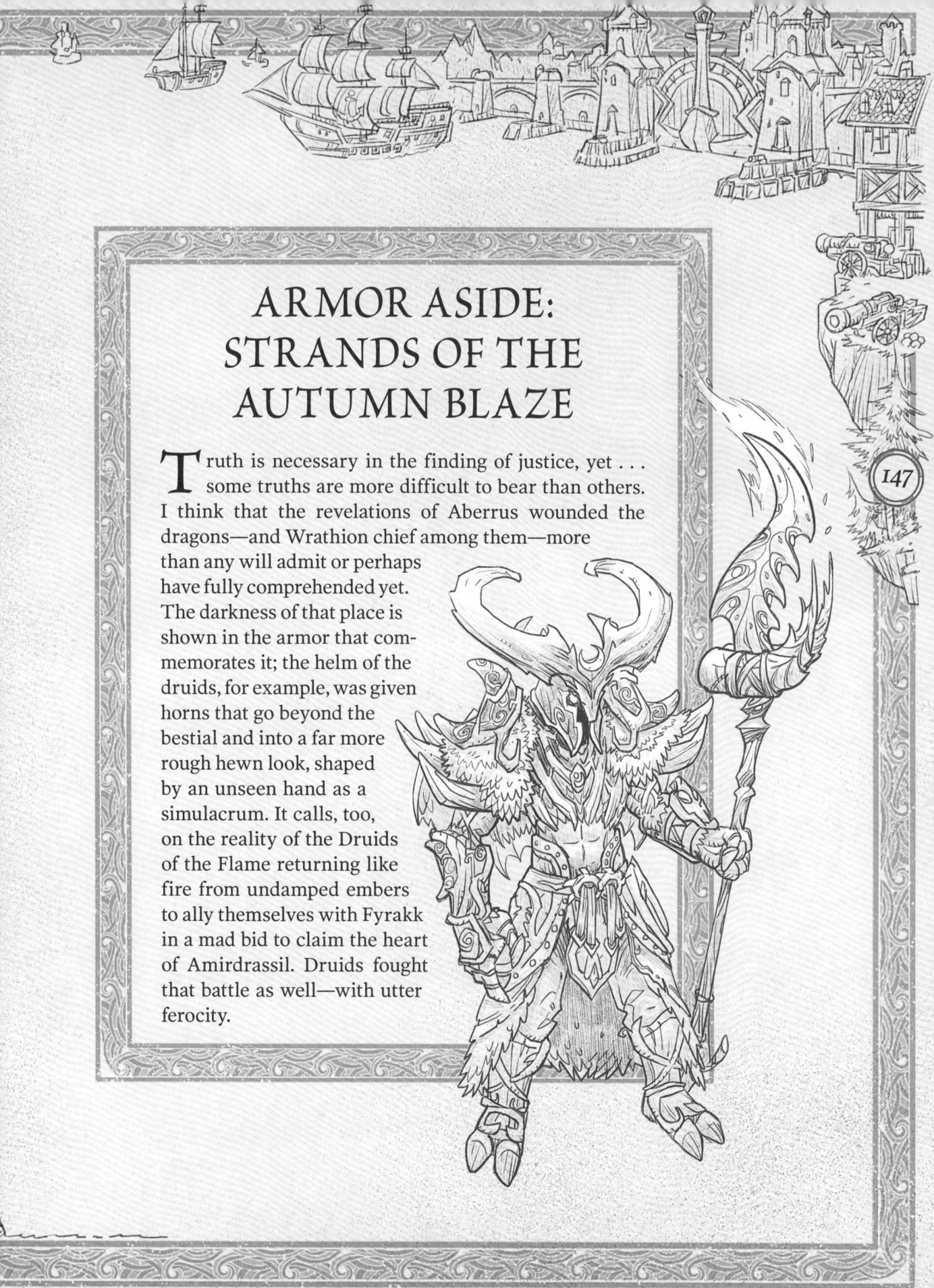

ARMOR ASIDE: STRANDS OF THE AUTUMN BLAZE

Truth is necessary in the finding of justice, yet ... some truths are more difficult to bear than others. I think that the revelations of Aberrus wounded the dragons—and Wrathion chief among them—more than any will admit or perhaps have fully comprehended yet. The darkness of that place is shown in the armor that commemorates it; the helm of the druids, for example, was given horns that go beyond the bestial and into a far more rough hewn look, shaped by an unseen hand as a simulacrum. It calls, too, on the reality of the Druids of the Flame returning like fire from undamped embers to ally themselves with Fyrakk in a mad bid to claim the heart of Amirdrassil. Druids fought that battle as well—with utter ferocity.

EMERALD GARDENS

The Emerald Gardens put me in mind of Val'sharah—for good reason, as the home of the green dragonflight and the start of their path into the Emerald Dream. In that way, for all that it was populated by many dragons, the Emerald Gardens felt familiar. The whole of the gardens is beautiful, but my favorite place within it was the Leafy Repose, a peaceful little stream at the bottom of a waterfall, surrounded by soft grass. Lor'themar nudged me and suggested this might also be another place ideal for renewing our vows, and we held each other . . . until Wrathion cleared his throat to remind us that he was there.

The greater part of the Emerald Gardens lies upon an island called the Ancient Bough, which sits just offshore, protected from unwanted visitors by ancient wards set into stone pillars. The Ancient Bough is home to both the Dream Portal—which connects the green dragonflight to the Emerald Dream—and the dragonflight's Oathstone. The gardens and the gateway they guard survived multiple concerted attacks by the Primalists and the Druids of the Flame under Fyrakk's command. And as is their wont, they have regrown.

A little rude of us, I suppose, but how often does one get to tease a young dragon?

OHN'IRI SPRINGS

Knowing of the Nokhud's betrayals of the other centaur clans, I was curious to see the state of their home territory. It was a rocky, hilly place, though apparently it was like this before their rebellion was crushed. I could see, as one who has lived through a civil war and observed the damage it does to a city, that Nokhud Hold was much reduced. There stood quite a few abandoned dwellings, and most of the centaur there were either the very old, who regarded us warily, or the very young, who were quite curious about me and Lor'themar. The remaining adults, Wrathion noted, were those who had defected from their own clan rather than attack the Khanam Matra.

We stopped for a full day in the Ohn'iri Springs to the south across the plains. While Wrathion did not spend the whole of it there with us, he took his own turn in the heated pools, first in his visage and, later, in his drake form, taking up half an entire pool all his own and resting his chin on a geyser. We later came to understand that we were only allowed entrance here because we were guests of the Khanam Matra—and with Wrathion. We were quite grateful for the opportunity. There is a very raw beauty to the hot springs—the winding mineral formations look almost like gateways over the pools.

AMIRDRASSIL

From the coast, we saw the new World Tree, Amirdrassil, Crown of Harmony, towering high above the Dragon Isles. I must admit, it was tempting to steal away from our tour route and glimpse the majesty of the tree firsthand, but neither Lor'themar nor myself have yet had the honor to visit with our entourage. My love suggested that, to arrive without our full retinue, our own blessings and gifts for Tyrande and Malfurion, seemed a grave misstep, even in these quieter times. I look forward to standing among its glorious boughs in person soon, however, with my own wish for continued healing between our peoples.

If we settle on a hot springs vacation, we're better off going to Fizzsprings Resort in Tiragarde Sound. A tourist destination, yes, but it's also quite pretty and means vacationing without having to be careful about accidentally breaching traditions.

–XI–
THE AZURE SPAN

If the Ohn'ahran Plains is a place that feels like endless spring and summer, the Azure Span is caught between autumn and the chill dead of winter. Fitting for the blue dragonflight, the closer one gets to their seat of power, the deeper the snows and more gem-blue the ice.

When the dragons first returned to the forested portions of the Span, where the leylines betray their subterranean presence in caves studded with purple crystal, the gnolls had tapped into a dark magic of disease and rot to infect both plants and magic. That has since been cleansed, though the forest still smells faintly of rot. But, as the tuskarr reminded when they told us these stories, some decay is to be expected in all facets of nature and life.

THE AZURE VAULT

Of everywhere on the Dragon Isles, I was personally most excited about the Azure Vault. Not as a honeymoon spot, of course, but as a beacon for any scholar of magic. I was not prepared for its sheer beauty inside—nor how filled with life it was. Though the blue dragonflight is still quite small, Wrathion said that Kalecgos has made every effort to bring them together as a family, and it shows in the warmth and activity within the Vault.

Most striking was the garden that Malygos, long before his madness, had planted for Sindragosa. That garden has been made a fitting memorial for two lovers torn apart by tragedy, with an arcane projection of a poem written long ago by Divo Songscale that recorded the tale of their love. Lor'themar and I sat amongst the arcane eddies and plants whose leaves rang like bells, and he read the poem to me. It made my wish to tear into the libraries less pressing—and it helped that Kalecgos promised that I could return whenever I liked.

I found out when we went to Camp Antonidas that the poem had been in fragments, scattered about the ruins. After learning of their existence, Noriko the All-Remembering gathered them together in a book.

ISKAARA

The tuskarr village of Iskaara sits on the far western shore of the Azure Span, on a somewhat incongruous ice floe—though it of course makes sense why the tuskarr would then make themselves a home there. It was a cozy and homey place, as most tuskarr settlements are, and they nearly drowned us in their local specialty soup, though in a very friendly way. I think Lor'themar was sloshing a bit when he excused himself to go look at the fishing boat the village artisans were in the process of building. I stayed by the fire with Wrathion, rapt by the endless stream of tales the village elders had to tell; listening closely, one could tease out quite a bit of information about local magic. Eventually I excused myself to find Lor'themar, pleased to see the utter joy on his face as one of the shipwrights offered him a chisel after demonstrating the proper tuskarr technique for wielding it.

"Going to join him?" Wrathion asked, amused.

I told him that I didn't need to, and realized it was so. To have him near was enough. We did not need to be acting always in concert for this time to be precious.

VAKTHROS

Vakthros sits upon a massive confluence of magic; I could all but taste it in the air as we approached the summit. The sign of the Primalists' siege upon the tower remains in the approach. The great tunnel melted through glacier and rock remains; it is being slowly filled again with ice, but it will take many centuries to be buried once more. Even with Raszageth gone, the blue dragonflight remains vigilant. There were a few Kirin Tor scholars here, invited by Kalecgos to study with members of his flight, and I had a lovely, if short, conversation with them.

ARMOR ASIDE: WRAPPINGS OF THE WAKING FIST

Monks, too, were among the champions who helped slay Raszageth in the Vault of the Primals. While I would have thought monks, with their swift movement, to be more suited to a look of air, they wear the strength of primal earth quite well. Of all types of warriors, I am given to understand their training emphasizes the grounding of the feet and center. An impressive artistic achievement, too, for the armor smiths to incorporate earth while keeping the armor light and lithe.

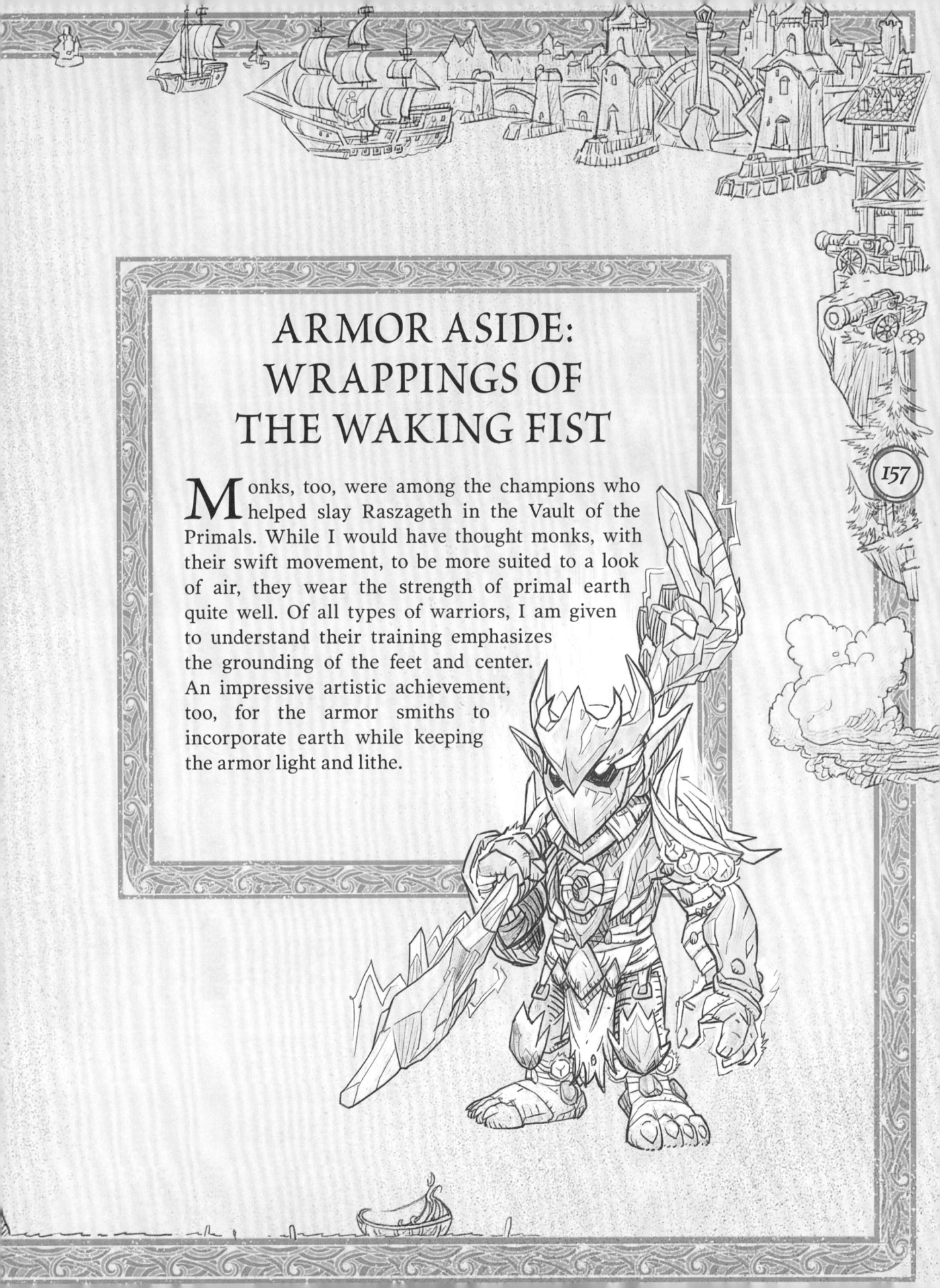

WINTERPELT HOLLOW

We passed through Imbu when traveling between the Azure Vault and Vakthros. It is not the most populous of the tuskarr villages in the Azure Span, but it is home to a massive stone carving that the tuskarr call their elder. If one looks closely, it appears to have been lovingly and recently repaired; the village was overrun by Primalists and its people driven away during that war.

We received a cautious yet still warm welcome at Winterpelt Hollow. The furbolgs there only recently have decided to speak with outsiders, in large part due to being helped by Horde and Alliance adventurers when they were attacked and captured by the Primalists. There were just a few in the village who spoke our language, but over the course of a meal with them, I made excellent strides in learning their tongue.

The deep Misty Canyon—so named because the river at its depths is perpetually shrouded in mist—forms part of the border between the Azure Span and Thaldraszus. It is half spanned by a broken bridge, which Wrathion said he'd been told was once a bustling thoroughfare before the dragons left the island. The bridge is something Kalecgos hopes to restore someday, though likely not for some time, as other matters require more urgent attention.

The Cobalt Assembly, while not in possession of as impressive a library as the Azure Vault, was quite a treat to visit for similar reasons—and I think Lor'themar enjoyed it even more. The blue dragons of the Cobalt Assembly had training grounds there, and he excused himself to terrorize a few of their younger drakonids at the archery butts while I was discussing the crafting of arcane objects with several of their enchanters. While the complex of buildings is another that shows the scars of both time and the depredations of the Sundered Flame, it is being renovated swiftly.

Before leaving the Azure Span, we paused for a last look at Camp Antonidas, which had been a Kirin Tor base of operations when the isles were first welcoming outsiders. The Kirin Tor have long since ceded it back to the snows; the mages who remain are staying much more comfortably at the Azure Vault itself, the Cobalt Assembly, or even Vakthros. But Lor'themar took this chance to search out the poetry fragments that had been collected in the gardens of the Vault, treating it as something of a team scavenger hunt that we conducted while holding hands.

We, too, have been so separated. Though I hope for a far happier ending for us.

–XII–
THE FORBIDDEN REACH

The small, northernmost set of islands comprise the Forbidden Reach, the home of the dracthyr. Though I wonder if "home" in this sense is a misnomer; it is where they were imprisoned at the whim of Neltharion for thousands of years, where he cruelly shaped them into his personal army. All the same, we were honored when Wrathion told us we'd been invited to see it by the dracthyr themselves.

MORQUT VILLAGE

Morqut Village is the entrance into the Forbidden Reach, though it is located on a small islet just off its coast. The tuskarr have been here for some time, fishing the waters, though they were temporarily driven from their home by Raszageth's storms. Now, the tuskarr still run their fishing boats, but they've built several more houses for the use of visitors, since so many now travel the interior of the once-forbidden islet.

CALDERA OF THE MENDERS

A low caldera that still speaks of its recent eruption with steaming, sulfur-smelling hot springs, the Caldera of the Menders is a place simultaneously beautiful and hellish. The Support Creche is located on one of its shores, a place where the Healing Wings dracthyr who wield the regenerative powers of the Emerald Dream were housed and trained. The creche is filled with poison; I know not if this is caused by a breakdown of some sort or if it was always like that as another of Neltharion's cruel testing grounds.

After all I have seen of Neltharion's legacy, I would tend to believe the latter. He was . . . calculating and insidious, long before he was Deathwing. And we both know how easily hidden such evil can be. We've had similar injustices in our midst and only found out about them too late . . .

FROSTSTONE VAULT

Froststone Vault looks like nothing so much as a cathedral only lightly touched by the depredations of time, a strange sight in the Forbidden Reach. It seems a very off choice for a prison . . . but so, too, does the Tomb of Sargeras. Inside are the remnants of books and arcane equipment, being studied by scholars of the Dragonscale Expedition. I presume Raszageth was held here not because it was built to house her but because it had the necessary arcane energies for such a binding.

STORMSUNDER CRATER

Stormsunder Crater is home to a beautiful lake; it's almost easy to forget what geological violence must have created such a deep well and its spires of rock frozen in some moment of explosion or impact. It seems the shape of the crater yields unique air currents—we saw many a dracthyr soaring about it. The entrance to the War Creche is not far from its outer rim, now a testing ground filled with lava spiders and other monsters.

OLD WEYRN GROUNDS

The Old Weyrn Grounds are filled with ruins and thunder lizards, though bands of researchers from the Dragonscale Expedition still comb through them for information, guarded by dracthyr. One of the dracthyr, led by Scalecommander Emberthal, told us that they had decided as a people to let the thunder lizards have these buildings. They have similarly chosen to seal away Dragonskull Island, a place where they were . . . tortured, to put it nicely, as a means of testing.

I have never seen a people so determined to forge their own path while remembering the lessons of their history. I hope that the dragons are proud to count them as allies and friends.

ZARALEK CAVERN

Wrathion took us back to the Ohn'ahran Plains, to lead us into the great cavern beneath the isle on the same road he had first traveled himself. This time, we went down the twisting path of Iridikron's Gambit—a feat of controlled flight that Lor'themar enjoyed far more than I did, judging by his whooping shouts—and into the great open space beneath. Zaralek Cavern is a wonder all its own, a strange world of rock that has never seen the sunlight, lit only by lava floes or luminescent crystals.

THE THROUGHWAY

The Throughway is the relatively low-clearance (and by that, I mean one might still fly a proto drake, but it is not as expansive as Zaralek proper) arm of the cavern that was once a dead end. Now, Iridikron's Gambit cuts into it, so that our first sight of Zaralek was floor-to-ceiling columns of luminescent crystals that we flew between. Immediately outside the Throughway is Deephollow Lake, a glowing pool filled with mineral-heavy water, blind fish, and strange artifacts. Wrathion remarked that Kalecgos is quite obsessed with the lake and its odd artifacts. Apparently, "He needed a hobby."

Past the lake lies Nal ks'kol, a titan facility that Neltharion used as a resource for his experiments; Oathbinder, the artifact he used to control the dracthyr, came from here. Now, the halls echo with researchers, though they are careful not to disturb the relics of the ancient dragons, including a fragment of Galakrond's claw. With those relics now rests the broken remains of Oathbinder, with a plaque that reads: A Reminder That We Will Not Kneel Again.

More of a journeyman, really. But the snails are far more interesting than you might think . . .

GLIMMEROGG

Glimmerogg is one of two towns in the cavern, the farthest from the Throughway. Its air is filled with luminescent motes (the glowing snot I produced when next I blew my nose is something I shall have to tell Oculeth about) that lend the humble buildings a sort of fairy charm. Really, it's more of a snail racing track where people sleep between bets than anything else. It took about two pints of mosswater and an hour of conversation for Lor'themar to become an expert on the sport and win several bets.

Nearby Loamm is a small town, quite literally. It is well both Lor'themar and I have had practice visiting goblin and vulpera dwellings, so we knew to duck as we went in and out of doors. While the niffen themselves are rather friendly, Wrathion told us that they were once even friendlier—and had fewer guard towers and shelters. Fyrakk attacked their town and slew many of their people with gouts of shadowflame. But rather than fleeing, the niffen followed their natures, rebuilt, and dug in for safety.

The niffen are also the only people who can tell me that I smell nice and not have me find it odd or offensive, due to their reliance on scent rather than sight to navigate the world.

Well, you did after the first time I bumped my head.

Other than me.

VIRIDIAN THRONE

Of the crystal formations in the cavern, the most impressive is the massive column among a veritable field of large crystals that the locals call the Viridian Throne. Every now and then a large collection of crystals gets itself together and begins stomping around until it's once more knocked down to size by an adventurer—the Viridian King. Though I am not certain if the monstrous "king" came first in naming or the throne itself.

ARMOR ASIDE: LEGACY OF OBSIDIAN SECRETS

I know some of the horrors that the champions of the Horde discovered inside Aberrus . . . but for the dracthyr who had barely begun to join our ranks, it must have been an even more difficult journey of revelation. Aberrus, after all, is where they were created, where they were bound to Neltharion. Of all who fought in those halls, they perhaps deserve the commemoration of their battle the most, and I hope they take the armor made for them as a triumph of strength, growth, and survival rather than a memory of pain.

ABERRUS

The reports I had heard of Neltharion's laboratory, Aberrus, did not do the sheer horror of the place justice. Wrathion stayed close by as we walked through the halls; while the old laboratory has been mostly cleared out, there are still occasional djaradin forays as they search for their missing elders, and the scars of the Sundered Flame have not been completely healed.

Wrathion was the most sober I had ever seen him as he gave us a tour through what I soon came to realize was his private nightmare—one not as ever-present as it might have once been, but I know well how some shadows never leave us. He explained how the elders whom the djaradin still seek had been here—only drained of their essence. How they had gone through the laboratory room by room to destroy experiments, still floating in agonized half life in tubes. Knowing what I do of his origins, Lor'themar and I each rested a hand on his arms, but we did not speak. Sometimes, words are woefully insufficient.

"It isn't just that," Wrathion finally explained. "The whispers are still here. Even if they have no power over me, I still come back more often than I should, to test myself."

That certainly explained the odd headache I'd begun to have, pressing at the back of my eyes.

"If it's any comfort, I feel it too," Lor'themar offered.

Wrathion laughed. "I'd rather you didn't."

At my urging, he took us into the depths, to the Edge of Oblivion. Part was pure curiosity, for me, as I have always wanted to poke my nose into places I shouldn't. But part . . . I wondered at some confirmation of the strange feelings I'd had in other places where there'd been rumors of "whispers."

It was the same.

GAZE OF NELTHARION

I never would have thought sitting atop a tower overlooking a blazing lake of lava would be soothing, but compared to our venture into Aberrus...

Lor'themar took a flask of mead he'd acquired somewhere in Kul Tiras from his pocket and offered me a bracing sip, though I made quite the face at how utterly sweet it was.

"You would think, with Raszageth and Fyrakk dead, there'd be more peace here. The shadowflame's been extinguished, as far as Ebyssian can tell." Wrathion's apparent frustration was a poor mask for his unease. "And Neltharion's long gone too. It's no worse than it was, but ... it's no better, either."

"Some shadows are so deep, they leave a lasting impression on the world," Lor'themar said.

I thought of how, too, the loa Bwonsamdi's chamber at the center of his Necropolis is called the Edge of Oblivion, and how it had also left me unsettled. "It is a window into some greater darkness," I finally said. "And a window can be looked through from either side."

–XIII–
THALDRASZUS

Thaldraszus is a lovely place of forests and craggy, near continuous mountains. It makes sense that the dragons made such a place the location for their capital. It is a pleasure to sail through the clear skies, pleasantly above what would be a nightmare of winding paths on foot. It is also where the bronze dragonflight has made its home, far to the south, near the border with the Azure Span.

I ought to have known you would be a daredevil as soon as someone gave you wings.

Hush, you're the one who keeps challenging me to races!

VALDRAKKEN

After the rather chilling end to our foray into Zaralek, Wrathion decided that we ought to go to Valdrakken, which is as close to the antithesis of Aberrus as might exist. I was happy to be back into the light and air—and bustle.

Valdrakken is as lively and populous a city as any in the Horde—or Alliance, I would daresay—with its own merchants and restaurants and streets, though the streets of Valdrakken are both on the ground and in the air.

There is a rhythm that all cities share no matter the culture, underlying like a deep heartbeat made by so many people of any kind occupying the same space. In that way, Valdrakken felt so familiar, at times I could nearly forget that most of those around me were dragonkind in all its myriad forms, dragons and drakonids and dracthyr . . . until a dragon burst into their true shape and took to the skies.

You are far too good at reading me. Truly, we are a matched pair.

SEAT OF THE ASPECTS

I had said there would be no work, as we were on vacation, and in my hypocrisy, it was a dictum that I had broken several times in Zandalar. (Though from Lor'themar's occasional guilty little twitch, I surmised he had done the same in Kul Tiras.) After Aberrus, both Lor'themar and I had much to mull over. We might have left it all unsaid were it not unthinkable to come to the city of the Aspects without at least politely saying hello to the regents themselves.

It was, regrettably, a meeting with far more business to it than I had wanted. Not even for the petty sake of my dreamed-of vacation, but for the sake of Azeroth.

The Aspects shared what news they had, taking turns to impart what each had the most knowledge of. We had been aware of the war with the Primalists and the defeat of both Raszageth and Fyrakk, though they offered far more detail than any reports either of us had read. Vyranoth, an Incarnate, joining with the dragons was . . . surprising, but we have all seen in the past few years how former enemies can become cherished allies.

More disturbing was the information about the final Incarnate, Iridikron, who had vanished. He'd last been seen with a device that held the essence of the ancient first proto-dragon, Galakrond; since then, it seemed that he'd given that device and the essence within to one only known as the Harbinger. Considering the feelings of the Incarnates, there is little doubt there will be some attack coming aimed at anything titan-touched on Azeroth. What might come from the essence of Galakrond is a mystery as yet, but the dragons generally agreed that nothing good could come of it for their kind. When we told them of what we'd heard in Zandalar and Kul Tiras, respectively, the mood only darkened further. Kalecgos promised to speak with Khadgar immediately; other than that, there was little to add.

We left the meeting with much to think on . . . and were promptly interrupted by Wrathion briskly clapping his hands together when we began to speak of it. "Nothing either of you can do about this now," he said. "So I'll play the dutiful friend and get you back to doing vacation things."

Which meant a tour of the city, it turned out.

THE ARTISAN'S MARKET

The Artisan's Market of Valdrakken lacks the frenetic business of the Grand Bazaar of Dazar'alor, but it is a unique treasure in its own way. The number of artisans, each an expert in their own craft, gathered there from so many corners of the world . . . it is unlike any assemblage I have ever seen. It has become a place where anyone can come and put in an order to have . . . anything made, really. Knowledge seems to flow even more freely than money; no wonder it has so quickly become a destination for apprentices and journeymen in the various crafts.

And if one is looking for something that doesn't exist,
I daresay the artisans will invent it before too long.

FALLINGWATER OVERLOOK

After wandering the Artisan's Market for hours, we decided to enjoy a meal, just the two of us. Lor'themar, ever the listener, had collected enough word of mouth to direct us to the Fallingwater Overlook—the nicest restaurant I've eaten at in quite some time. (And even longer if we don't count occasions when I was working in some capacity.) The proprietor offered to clear the restaurant for us for a price. Tempting, but it was strangely calming to be just one patron among many. Lor'themar and I ate at our table outside, where we could enjoy the many waterfalls of the Cascades—no work, no interruptions, and no rush.

There was a teahouse nearby (though I didn't catch its name) that had some fascinating blends to offer. I bought a few and had them boxed up to be sent back to Suramar City. As we walked back into the city proper, Lor'themar suggested that for our next dinner, we ought to try the Ruby Feast, another restaurant fervently commended to him.

Now this is a resort!
SERENE DREAMS SPA

After all the traveling we had done, we took a day to luxuriate in the hot springs of the Serene Dreams Spa and enjoy the various treatments. The manager's manager, a very sweet green dragon named Quilius, even talked us into trying their mud mask. Lor'themar, ever the charmer even with his face covered in expensive mud, had the story from a few of the employees about the spa's rather rocky beginning, when it was overtaken by a Primalist and her supporters, who stirred up all the steam and fire elementals until they furiously began attacking guests. It's certainly recovered well since then.

VAULT OF THE INCARNATES

After the peace of Valdrakken, the Vault of the Incarnates felt a dark and violent place that put me rather in mind of the Vault of the Wardens. Unsurprising, as both have and still do serve as prisons for that which would destroy Azeroth as she exists. Wrathion grimly noted that when Iridikron is finally caught, he will be destroyed rather than being brought back to the Vault.

ALGETH'AR ACADEMY

While the Vault of the Incarnates had been a rather sobering reminder that there were still threats we all must face together, Algeth'ar Academy was a pure joy. Since its reopening, it has burgeoned with students from across Azeroth; while we were there, a few nightborne I had recommended months previously made certain to greet me. (I know, as well, Oculeth has made a trip here—it was one of the reasons I was so delighted to go myself. I had to outdo his Talon Toss score if afforded the chance to do so.) Headteacher Doragosa offered to give us a modified version of their tour for prospective students—and Lor'themar, a wicked twinkle in his eye, suggested we make it a competition.

I, of course, pledged myself to the blue dragonflight. Lor'themar chose the red dragonflight. And then he led me on a merry chase through the various exercises and games. I had no trouble keeping up with him until the Talon Toss arena, at which point he proceeded to make such ridiculous faces and pull such tricks that I was all but helpless laughing. So he did win the day, but I maintain that it was through cheating. A good thing the stakes were only the same as our poetry contest—a kiss.

I beg your pardon! I took a tactical advantage where I saw it. Not against the rules at all.

"Lish Llrath," my love.
When in Valdrakken . . .

TYRHOLD

To say that Tyrhold is an architectural marvel is perhaps unnecessary; all titan facilities have that quality to them. But Tyrhold is certainly the most intact and well-maintained titan facility I've seen—Lor'themar said even more so than Ulduar, as it's not been subjected to attacks and fighting. While I'm not one to obsess over aqueducts, even I could see the ones at Tyrhold were a marvel.

With the aberrant guardians pacified, Wrathion was free to show us around at his leisure, though he instead put Watcher Koranos in charge of the tour. Perhaps for the best, as Koranos answered all the questions that I had (as best he could, though he is a guardian rather than a scholar of magic) with the patience of stone. We were allowed, too, to see the Halls of Infusion, which supply water to the Ruby Life Pools, among other things.

THE VEILED OSSUARY

The graveyard of dragons has the same stillness as any other graveyard, even if the bones are different. The story of Sindragosa and Malygos still weighed on my mind. While the Azure Vault was where their essences had passed fully beyond, there was still some part of me that wished to see their names memorialized together, with Lor'themar by my side. It rings true, how love can endure past death . . . and that no matter how much time two people might have together, it is still never enough. I also bid farewell to Senegos; I had not known him well when he lived in Azsuna, but I heard of his departure not long after the Dragon Isles were opened and knew it to be a loss of great wisdom for us all. I wish that there had been time before that for me to know him . . . but time is ever fleeting. A reminder, then, to take the moments I can, lest they slip away.

Wrathion had wandered off for quite some time before he rejoined us; Lor'themar joked that he must have been giving us time alone. Wrathion shrugged in that careless way of his, but he was all sobriety when he said: "I come here to make certain I've not forgotten the name of anyone who Neltharion slew."

"My friend," Lor'themar told him, "it isn't your burden to bear." Nor to any in the current black dragonflight, really. Wrathion wasn't even hatched at that time.

"I know," was Wrathion's reply. "But it's mine to remember, so that it never happens again."

And the winds over that area are the most complicated and thrilling that Wrathion showed us!

THE TEMPORAL CONFLUX

The home of the bronze dragonflight is an incongruous outpouring of shining, windswept sand that splays out against the southern mountain range of Thaldraszus; its shifting patterns never leave that area, for all they constantly remake themselves into mysterious ridges.

We were offered the opportunity—due to our stations, I think—to peer at the past. A valuable offer to clarify memory. I . . . declined, though I think it surprised Lor'themar. The stories they told us were strange enough—such as an alternate timeline where everyone and everything living was a murloc.

It did indeed. You're always so curious about everything.

Mrghlglgrlrgrlgr!!

Lor'themar, I will—

I might like to unweave the magic to try to understand it, but . . . I have begun to understand that it is best to see what is before me than trouble myself with what has passed.

ARMOR ASIDE: UNDERLIGHT CONJURER'S BRILLIANCE

At first glance, the armor made for mages who braved the halls of Aberrus seems incongruously bright, considering the darkness within—and so much of it brought about by terrible experiments. But as a mage myself, the fierce light of arcane magic that shines in these robes is a shout of defiance, that for every ill this beautiful and powerful tool of ours is used to accomplish, we shall push back the darkness a thousandfold with the bright ferocity of knowledge and hope.

GARDENS OF UNITY

At first, I thought Wrathion was simply taking us back to Valdrakken, which made me wonder if perhaps there was more ill news, but he seemed far too lighthearted (or as lighthearted as Wrathion allows himself to be). He would not tell us *where* we were going, and he only seemed more amused each time I asked.

Our destination was the Gardens of Unity, a place of winding paths and flowers and soft grass. While we saw many gardens in our travels, this one celebrated the flights coming together, with each flight represented in some way. The reason for his happiness wasn't too hard to gather, since there were quite a few other dragons in the gardens, including the dragons Wrathion called his brothers, Ebyssian and Sabellian. It seemed that a new portion of the gardens was being opened—one that represented the black dragonflight.

Lor'themar and I were quick to tell all the black dragons who had come how pleased we were to be invited. Their portion of the gardens was very different from the others, but very *them*—a garden of rocks, each carefully placed such that it built its internal harmony. (Including a large and inviting flat rock on which dragons would feel welcome to sun themselves.)

The Gardens of Unity was such an inviting place . . . no, it wasn't even that. It was after traveling so long, and thinking, and missing Lor'themar so, I didn't see a need to travel any farther in our search. It was enough to be here, with him. It could have been anywhere, so long as I was far enough from my responsibilities that I could let myself be . . . me. But amongst the gardens, in the shadow of Valdrakken, it certainly didn't hurt as a place to honeymoon.

Except then we heard . . . her.

I agree.

I think, now as I pick over each detail in my memory, searching for any tiny crumb of information I could possibly glean . . . I think Wrathion heard it first. Our friend masks his distress well, always, but Lor'themar and I had spent such time with him over this vacation of ours, and I daresay been privileged with such trust from him that we'd gotten to see past his normal amused and laconic air. I remember, then, the corner of his eyes going tight as I began to say something to him, one of his hands twitching up as if he might reach for his head, struck by a sudden ache.

And then it had me. I recognize, now, something of those whisperings I had heard before, but it had become an inescapable scream, a blinding light that seared my mind rather than my eyes:

"Hear my call, Thalyssra. Know me."

I found myself half-fallen into Lor'themar's arms, and he none too steady on his feet, his teeth gritted against what I had little doubt was a pounding echo in his head to match my own. I did not need to ask if he had heard and felt this same call; it was plain on his face. "I don't know," I answered, to a question he didn't need to ask. "But we must find out." Already, in my mind, I was building the portals that would take us to our cities.

There was so much to be said. Regrets, what-ifs, worries, fears, plans already forming, all our tenuous peace shattered in one strange, frenetic moment. But both of us know our duty and what our people and our world need of us. And thus, I chose to say the only thing that mattered: "I love you."

And I, you. Always.

My light,

Even now, I am cursing that there was no time for us to say our proper goodbyes. A hasty kiss before diving into separate portals hardly counts. And . . . I cannot imagine how you must feel. I was happy to spend what time with you that we had, but we never got to enjoy the proper honeymoon you envisioned.

I will hold out hope that someday soon we will have that chance again, just the two of us, with no work to interfere. (And no Wrathion throwing a mouthy fool into our cake . . . Though I think when we have our vows renewed, we should have a second cake made. Either we'll need it, or he'll think it's a hilarious joke.)

I know well that disappointment is part of life, but I could do with a bit less disappointment and a bit more time with you. May I see you soon . . . and hopefully not amid battle.

With all my love,
Lor'themar

My love,

I know that this will make you shake your head and chuckle (you're already doing it, I wager) but . . . I think we did have our honeymoon, after all. Our entire journey across the Dragon Isles was all I could have asked for . . . because I was with you.

I only wish that it had not taken so much time apart for me to understand that point, that it was never about where we were or what we were doing, but that we were simply together. It seems even I am not immune to the vagaries and pressures of expectation. But I should have known that seeking perfection is often the path to destroy what one would perfect.

I do not think we will escape this war we both feel coming, but we know who we are fighting it for. Our people, always, but for each other. For what we have already been, and what we will be, together. Love is not easy, but it is worth fighting for, every day.

Dream of me, as I dream of you.

Your Thalyssra

My light,

I'm relieved to know we've now had a honeymoon, and a good one, even if I didn't quite realize it at the time. (I tease. Every best moment of that trip I could recount is one spent with you.)

However . . . what about a second honeymoon? I'd almost forgotten that I picked up this flier at . . . I'm not certain where. It survived the trip in my luggage, so it must be fate.

TIRED OF GLOOMY SKIES AND BOILED VEGETABLES?

SEE BEAUTIFUL TEL' ABIM

THE ISLAND OF ISLANDS

Reasonably priced resort packages—drinks included!

Try our special banana bomb,
guaranteed to erase even the strongest memories!

Dancing boys and girls and octo

Well, how could I say no, if the drinks are included . . . and so are you?

World of Warcraft

Artist Index for Exploring Azeroth: Islands & Isles

Francesca Baerald:
Cover Border, 5, 7, 189, 192

Joseph Lacroix:
Interior Borders, 16, 35, 48, 70, 84, 99,
111, 126, 136, 147, 157, 169, 183

Mats Myrvold: 143

N-iX Game & VR Studio
Artist: Taras Susak
Art Manager: Sergii Gotsman
22, 23, 24, 46, 59, 72-73, 74, 112-113,
135, 141, 145, 184-185

Surfside3D:
CEO: Maksim Gaidei
Art Director: Andrey Kultyshev
Lead 2D Artist: Uliana Suldina
Artists: Tagir Akhmadeev, Boris borich Gerasimov,
Oleg Markelov, Evgenii Shvenk, Olga Slyusareva,
Maria Trofimova, Alina Ulashchuk
HR Manager: Anastasia Mordvinova
Project Managers: Mikhail Izmailov, Marina Kozlova
10-11, 13, 14-15, 20-21, 27, 28-29, 33, 36-37, 40-41, 43, 44-45, 51,
54-55, 57, 63, 65, 66-67, 77, 78, 81, 86, 90-91, 93, 96-97, 101, 105,
107, 109, 114, 117, 119, 120-121, 124, 129, 132-133, 138-139,
148-149, 150, 153, 155, 161, 162-163, 164, 166-167, 173,
174-175, 176-177, 178-179

© 2024 Blizzard Entertainment, Inc.
Blizzard and the Blizzard Entertainment logo are trademarks or registered trademarks of Blizzard Entertainment, Inc. in the US or other countries.

Published by Titan Books, London, in 2024.

No part of this publication may be reproduced, stored in a retrieval system, or transmitted, in any form or by any means without the prior written permission of the publisher, nor be otherwise circulated in any form of binding or cover other than that in which it is published and without a similar condition being imposed on the subsequent purchaser.

Blizzard Entertainment does not have any control over and does not assume any responsibility for author or third-party websites or their content.

Adobe Stock Photo Cedits: TK

TITAN BOOKS

A division of Titan Publishing Group Ltd
144 Southwark Street
London SE1 0UP

www.titanbooks.com

Find us on Facebook: www.facebook.com/titanbooks

Follow us on X: @TitanBooks

A CIP catalogue record for this title is available from the British Library.

ISBN: 9781803368610

Manufactured in China

Print run 10 9 8 7 6 5 4 3 2 1

WRITTEN BY
Alex Acks

EDITED BY
Eric Geron, Chloe Fraboni

DESIGNED BY
Jessica Rodriguez

PRODUCED BY
Brianne Messina, Amber Proue-Thibodeau

LORE CONSULTATION BY
Courtney Chavez, Sean Copeland, Damien Jahrsdoerfer

GAME TEAM CONSULTATION BY
Steve Aguilar, Ely Cannon, Steve Danuser, Stacey Phillips, Chris Metzen, Korey Regan

SPECIAL THANKS
Adamari Rodriguez

BLIZZARD ENTERTAINMENT

MANAGER, PUBLISHING
Peter Molinari

EDITORIAL SUPERVISOR
Chloe Fraboni

ASSOCIATE MANAGER, CONSUMER PRODUCTS
Chanee' Goude

SENIOR BRAND ARTIST
Corey Peterschmidt

SENIOR DIRECTOR, STORY & FRANCHISE DEVELOPMENT
Venecia Duran

ASSOCIATE MANAGER, CREATIVE DEVELOPMENT PRODUCTION
Jamie Ortiz

SENIOR MANAGER, WRITING & BOOKS
Matthew Cohan

PRODUCER, LORE
Ed Fox

SENIOR PRODUCER, BOOKS
Brianne Messina

LORE HISTORIAN LEAD
Sean Copeland

ASSOCIATE PRODUCER, BOOKS
Amber Proue-Thibodeau

ASSOCIATE HISTORIAN
Ian Landa-Beavers